I0813235

THROUGH THE GATES OF HELL

American Injustice at Guantanamo Bay

JOSHUA COLANGELO-BRYAN

HUMANITAS
MEDIA

"Those who would give up essential Liberty, to purchase a little temporary Safety, deserve neither Liberty nor Safety."

—Benjamin Franklin

CONTENTS

Chapter 1

HABEAS ON THE GATE

October 2004

"We'll be watching," the sergeant said, pointing at a video monitor inside Camp Echo's guard booth. "For your protection." The monitor showed a grainy image of a table and chairs in a small room. To the side of the room was a tiny cell, partially hidden behind a metal mesh wall. I was about to have my first meeting with a Guantanamo Bay detainee in a room just like that.

"You have any questions before you go in?" the sergeant asked.

I certainly did. Donald Rumsfeld, the secretary of defense, had said that the detainees were "among the most dangerous, best-trained vicious killers on the face of the earth." President George W. Bush had said that they had been "trying to kill Americans." General Richard Myers, the chairman of the Joint Chiefs of Staff, had said they would chew through hydraulic cables to bring down airplanes. I didn't buy that kind of rhetoric wholesale, but it wasn't hard to imagine that there were some nasty characters at Guantanamo. It was impossible not to wonder if I was about to meet one.

These questions had been on my mind for several months, ever since I had convinced management at my corporate law firm to represent six Bahraini detainees. According to a document the government provided us under court order, the thirty-one-year-old client I was about to see had received military training in Afghanistan, gone to Bosnia to fight, and been arrested in connection with a bombing in Saudi Arabia. A day earlier, on the small prop plane that ferried us to Guantanamo from Fort Lauderdale, I had read stories from the internet describing this man as an Al Qaeda recruiter. For a moment, I pictured myself sitting alone with a big, bearded, menacing Arab who would try to reach across the table for my throat.

Figuring the sergeant was asking if I had questions about protocol or logistics, I said no. A military guard escorted my interpreter, Karim, and me away from the centrally located guard booth and toward one of a series of small wooden buildings that were spread out around Camp Echo's gravel compound. The buildings were on short stilts, and despite resembling low-rent beach cabanas, each housed an interview room and cell like the one on the monitor. Beyond the buildings, and surrounding the camp, were several fifteen-foot-tall chain-link fences, each topped by razor wire and covered with a green tarp, evidently to keep people from looking in or out. We walked up to one of the buildings where a guard held the door slightly ajar. I nodded to him and, more tentatively than I might have liked, went inside.

Jaber Mohammed sat at a table, flanked by guards. When he saw me, his face broke into a warm smile. As I walked toward him, I sized him up, a habit I had developed as a kid on New York subways and school playgrounds. I guessed he was about five foot six and 140 pounds—not exactly a gladiator's build. I started to feel a little embarrassed for worrying about meeting a vicious trained killer. Jaber had a beard but the rest of him didn't match my overwrought mental image.

One of Jaber's ankles was shackled to a bolt that was attached to the floor. He struggled to get halfway to his feet. We shook hands.

"Assalamu alaikum," I said. Having exhausted my Arabic, I looked to Karim for help, "I'm Josh Colangelo. I'm your lawyer. It's very good to meet you."

"Hello, I am Jaber," he said in heavily accented English before shaking hands with Karim and switching to Arabic.

"Thank you for coming. I have been waiting for your visit. Please sit," he said, gesturing to the table. It seemed Jaber was doing his best to be a gracious host despite his shackles and our inhospitable surroundings.

Once we sat down, the guards left.

"Do I understand correctly, then, that you received my letter?" I asked, referring to correspondence I had sent two months earlier. Jaber nodded.

"As I said in my letter, I'm a lawyer with a firm in New York. Your brother Amir asked my law firm to represent you. Or to be more precise, he asked an American human rights lawyer who was in Bahrain to represent you. That lawyer asked me if my firm would take the case."

"When did you find out that you would be seeing me today?" I inquired.

"This morning they told me I was moving, but they did not say why."

"I'm sorry about that. Do you normally stay somewhere else?"

"Yes, I am in Camp 5. This is worse than Camp 5." Jaber gestured to the cell two feet away from us, sealed off from the rest of the room by the same sort of metal mesh wall I'd seen on the monitor.

I didn't know much about Camp 5, but Jaber's observation was well taken. The cell next to us couldn't have been any smaller. The main section was as long as the concrete slab that served as a bed and no wider than five or six feet. The cell had another small area for a shower, but it was locked behind a heavy steel door. There was nothing in the room except the cell and our meeting area. Anyone spending a night there would be completely alone, except for the remarkably loud drone of an air conditioner that sounded like it was on its last legs.

"I'm sorry you have to stay in a place worse than usual just to see your lawyer."

Jaber smiled and waved his hand as if to say that I shouldn't worry about such inconveniences. Again, the gracious host.

One thing I had been worrying about was whether Jaber would be able to trust a thirty-something, white, short-haired American who showed up at Guantanamo claiming to be his lawyer. It seemed likely that the only people fitting my description he had seen over the prior few years were guards, interrogators, and the like. Maybe he would think that this was just some CIA agent's ruse.

I attacked that issue first. "I thought it might be hard for you to believe that it was really Amir who sent me here. So I asked him to tell me a few personal details about you that only people close to you would know. Do you mind if I share those details?"

"No, please tell me."

"Amir said that when you were a child, your favorite beach was Half Moon Beach."

Jaber smiled as if savoring a memory. "Yes, Half Moon Beach," he said in English.

"Amir said that he can't wait to go there with you when you get home."

"Please tell him that I look forward to doing the same."

"Amir also told me that you loved the movie *Jumanji*." Jaber smiled again.

"I am a little embarrassed to say that I asked him if it was a Middle Eastern movie, and Amir had to tell me it's American."

Jaber laughed. "You don't know this movie?"

"No, I've never seen it."

I had googled the film and learned that it starred Robin Williams and was about kids playing a board game. It wasn't my kind of cinema, and it had struck me as an odd favorite for a supposed jihadist.

"You should see it. It's very good," Jaber said earnestly.

"I'll have to watch it when I get home."

As we spoke, I wondered what personal details I would tell a lawyer if my younger brother were detained thousands of miles from home by a foreign country's army. Maybe it would be about where we had played Little League baseball. Or maybe that whenever we played the card game spit as kids, the loser accused the winner of cheating.

I also was trying to remember if there was anything more from Amir to share. Several weeks earlier, the military had demanded that we agree to a set of access procedures as a precondition for our visit. One of the procedures allowed the military to review any materials we brought into our client meetings; it was a matter of national security, they said. The idea of giving an attorney-client-privileged meeting outline to our clients' jailer was unacceptable. So, rather than bringing notes, we decided to memorize the subjects we wanted to discuss. I had spent several hours on the plane ride down studying for that purpose and resisting fifth-grade impulses to write key phrases on my hand.

"Jaber, unless you have questions about what Amir told me, I would like to explain why we agreed to represent you."

"Yes, that would be good," he said.

I told him my firm had over six hundred lawyers with offices around the world. Jaber seemed impressed; I decided not to say that by New York standards, it wasn't that big. I told him we would represent all six Bahrainis at Guantanamo, and that a colleague of mine, senior to me, was with another client right then.

"I don't need to tell you that the government has classified you as an 'enemy combatant.' The government claims it can hold anyone it calls an enemy combatant in jail forever without a trial. The government claims that enemy combatants do not have any rights at all, but I guess you know that also."

Jaber smiled knowingly.

"Now, you might disagree, Jaber, but personally I don't think that's right."

He chuckled and nodded.

"If someone is facing life in jail, I believe the person deserves a fair hearing to determine if he has done something wrong. My law firm feels the same way, and that's why we agreed to represent you. It's as simple as that."

Prattling on about due process can be trite in normal conversation, but Jaber didn't seem to find my explanation clichéd. "I am very grateful to you and your law firm," he said.

"You're welcome, but we believe we have an obligation to provide legal help to people who wouldn't have it otherwise. We call it pro bono work, which means we aren't paid for what we do." For a minute I felt like I was trying to sell an idealistic law student on working for the firm because it had a social conscience.

"I am still grateful," Jaber said.

I told Jaber that before coming to the firm, I had been in Kosovo for two years working with the United Nations on war crimes and terrorism cases, and doing humanitarian work with an aid group (it had been two different stints, separated by a year at a law firm in Seattle). I felt he needed to know I hadn't spent my entire career sitting in a fancy office defending corporations. I might gain a little credibility. I didn't say so explicitly but much of my work had been on behalf of nominally Muslim, ethnic Albanians who had long suffered at the hands of Slobodan Milosevic and nominally Christian Serbs.

Kosovo was never the cause célèbre in the Muslim world that Bosnia or Afghanistan had been, but Jaber could be familiar with the situation there. As I spoke about the work I had done to get Albanian detainees transferred from prisons in Serbia proper to Kosovo, I felt like I was pandering a bit. I didn't mind when Jaber just nodded politely in response. *I'll skip that routine with the next client*, I thought.

"In your letter you said that there was a court case for the detainees. Can you explain this?" Jaber asked.

"Sure. In June of this year, the Supreme Court, the highest court in America, ruled that detainees at Guantanamo can bring court cases. Specifically, the Supreme Court said that detainees are entitled to bring habeas corpus petitions. A habeas petition is made by someone who is in jail. The petition requires the government to produce evidence in court showing there is a legitimate reason for holding the person. The person can respond to the government's evidence and submit his own. Then a court decides if the person should be held in jail."

I spoke slowly and in deliberately simple terms. I avoided idioms and contractions. I let Karim translate after each sentence. It was hard enough to explain the Supreme Court's ruling to Americans who spoke English as a first language. And I remembered times in Kosovo when people would speak in long, disorganized paragraphs before giving an interpreter the chance to translate. It never worked well.

"But isn't the Supreme Court part of the government?" Jaber asked. "If the government says we have no rights, how can the Supreme Court say something else?"

"Wait," I said with mock exasperation. "Are you asking me hard questions already? Nobody told me I'd have to answer hard questions."

Jaber laughed. "Yes, I have many hard questions."

"Okay, let me try to answer. You're right that the Supreme Court is part of the government. But if I say that the government claims you have no rights, I'm talking about the president. The Supreme Court and the president are both part of the government, but they're separate. Under some circumstances, the Supreme Court can tell the president what to do."

Not knowing how much sense this would make to someone who grew up in a Middle Eastern monarchy, I drew a diagram, trying to illustrate the separation of powers doctrine. The visual arts have never been a strong suit, but Jaber seemed satisfied.

"So, I can make one of these . . . petitions?" he asked.

"Actually, we already brought habeas petitions for you and the other Bahrainis."

"Thank you. What evidence has the government shown to the court about me?"

"Well, nothing yet. We still have some preliminary issues to resolve, but we hope to have hearings relatively soon."

In fact, the government had just made a motion to have our petitions dismissed, arguing that the Supreme Court decision was simply a formality that did not give the detainees any rights. I decided against trying to explain motion practice just yet because we had already covered some nuanced ground, and I didn't want Jaber to think we were stopped in our tracks before even starting. There would be time to talk about those legal machinations later.

"I'd like to explain some other things about our work. In America, anything a lawyer and client talk about is confidential. The court has said that the right to confidentiality applies here. I will do everything I can to preserve that confidentiality, but unfortunately I can't guarantee it."

I pointed to the camera that was mounted on the ceiling. "The military said that the camera records only visual images, but I have no way to verify if that's true."

I gestured toward the impressive collection of wires that were attached to the walls of our meeting area. Some led to an intercom, some to a telephone, and some to a light fixture, but the purpose of others was harder to discern.

"I've been told that there is no listening device here. Without wanting to be paranoid, I can't be sure of that either."

I continued, "Also, the government says that anything you tell me is considered classified because it could relate to national security." This was from the access procedures we had been made to sign. "If information is considered classified, that means it cannot be disclosed to the public. It's secret."

"Anything I say is secret?" Jaber asked.

"Anything."

"Even if I just tell you that *Jumanji* is good?"

"Your movie reviews are secret."

"What if I say that my foot hurts?"

"Yeah, that's secret too," I said, shrugging my shoulders to distance myself from the legal position I was describing.

Jaber looked amused. "I must be very important to have so many secrets."

"You know what? Before the military would even let me come to Guantanamo to hear your secrets, I had to undergo an FBI background investigation. The FBI came to my apartment to talk to my girlfriend and neighbors, read my tax returns, and looked around my office. They did the same for Karim before they let him come with me."

The background check had felt entirely invasive at first, but there was no way around it for anyone wanting to go to Guantanamo. And the investigators ended up being retired FBI agents who were charming in an old-gumshoe sort of way. I actually enjoyed being interviewed by them, as the discussion quickly moved to their war stories. One of them smiled as he told me that the question "Does Josh live beyond his means?" had elicited laughs from everyone he asked—obviously he was talking to people familiar with my financially conservative style.

"So, you have lots of secrets, and the government knows everything about us," I told Jaber.

"I don't know which is worse," he said.

"And because everything you say is classified or secret, if I write down your words, my notes become secret. At the end of our meeting, I have to give my notes to the military. The military is not supposed to read them. It's supposed to send them to what is called a 'secure facility' in America, where I will be able to review them. But, again, I cannot guarantee my notes won't be read. So, if you want to say something that you don't want me to write down, please tell me.

"There may be times when I will want to disclose your words to the government of Bahrain or your family or maybe to the press. To do that, I will have to ask a special government team to review my notes to determine if they really are classified. That team is not supposed to share anything it sees with the lawyers who are representing the military in your court case. But, again, if there is something that you don't want me to show to the special government team, just let me know."

Could there be a worse way to convince a client who had been held incommunicado for nearly three years to be open and honest with a lawyer? Probably not, but Jaber needed to know these things.

Maybe if he understood the restrictions that had been imposed on us, he would be less likely to think I was some undercover agent.

He wasn't fazed. "I have nothing to hide."

Over the next three years, the only things that Jaber or other clients ever asked me not to write were the most personal details about themselves or their families.

I looked down and saw a plastic bag near my feet that I had forgotten about entirely. It was filled with stuff from Sahadi's, a Middle Eastern specialty shop in Brooklyn.

"Jaber, I realize it might threaten national security, but they let us bring in food. Would you like to eat something?"

"If you eat with me."

I took out baklava, dried fruit, date cookies, pistachios, and other things that had seemed likely to survive the daylong trip to Cuba. I motioned to Jaber to eat. He motioned to Karim and me to eat. The standoff lasted for a moment before everyone took something.

It seemed like a good time to find out if Jaber would be willing to tell me about himself.

"Jaber, if you don't know it already, you are going to find out that lawyers can be *really* boring. I'm sorry to say that your lawyer is no exception. Sometimes I ask very annoying questions until I get all the information I need. I don't do it to make people miserable. It's just that lawyers need to be very precise sometimes in what they say about their clients. How would you feel if I asked you some of those boring, annoying questions now?"

"Tell me what you want to know."

"Would you tell me about your family?" I hoped that letting him know he had control over our conversation might distinguish me from an interrogator. I also hoped that talking about family would be a safe place to start. It was.

"My grandfather was a tribal chief in Bahrain," Jaber said. "My father had a construction company in Saudi Arabia, where I grew up."

I knew that Jaber had joint Saudi Arabian–Bahraini citizenship. I had consulted a map before our visit and saw that Bahrain sits off the coast of Saudi Arabia in the Persian Gulf. The two countries are linked by the fifteen-mile King Fahd Causeway that spans the Gulf of Bahrain.

"I have several brothers and sisters. One of my sisters married a Bahraini prince. I was married when I was twenty-one, but my wife and I were divorced in 2000."

"I apologize for my ignorance, but is divorce common in Saudi?" I asked, thinking that it couldn't be.

"Before it was not, but it is more common now. My marriage was not good. I was very young, and there wasn't enough feeling in it."

"Divorce is hard."

"Were you divorced?" he asked.

"No, I've never been married, but my parents made everyone pretty miserable when they got divorced. I was a young kid." I skipped telling him that the culmination of that divorce was a multiyear, bicoastal custody fight involving courts, clandestine trips across the country, police, and a brief stay in foster care.

Jaber nodded and said that he had a nine-year-old daughter named Amal. He looked at the table for a moment or two, evidently thinking about her. Looking back up and with plaintive irony he said in English, "Don't worry, be happy," before going quiet again.

I remembered something else that Amir had told me and tried to break the silence. "Jaber, your brother said you like *molokhia*." It's a traditional Egyptian broth made from jute greens and eaten over rice and chicken.

He smiled, "My mother makes great molokhia."

"My girlfriend's family is Lebanese, and that's my favorite at their house."

"One day we will eat my mother's molokhia together. It may be different from the Lebanese style."

"I look forward to it."

Jaber thought for a moment. "Joshua is a Jewish name. Are you Jewish?"

The question caught me by surprise, and I had a sinking feeling that things were going to get anti-Semitic. It's not that I would have abandoned the case—I have heard plenty of well-heeled, paying clients say racist or sexist things—but I always lose a little enthusiasm when a client shows that side of himself.

"No, Joshua was just a popular name in the neighborhood where I grew up." I didn't really want to hear Jaber's response.

"Oh," he said, sounding slightly disappointed. "I heard the best lawyers were Jewish."

Quickly, and obviously for my benefit, he added, "But I'm sure you're good too."

My dad had told me once that there was a period when Italian-American mobsters who got arrested always asked for Jewish lawyers. I had no idea how that legal strategy might have migrated to Guantanamo, but I was relieved that Jaber was just checking my professional credentials.

It was getting toward noon, when our meeting was scheduled to end. The plan was to see Jaber for three more sessions, but I resisted telling him we were almost finished that day. We had been talking for several hours, and he seemed to be soaking up all the human interaction he could get. It felt almost cruel to leave. At around 11:50, I said I would have to go, but I would be back the next day. A minute later, a guard knocked on the door and yelled that our time was up. Jaber, Karim, and I kept talking until the guard opened the door and came in.

As I was stepping outside, I looked back to reassure Jaber that we would see him the next morning. He flashed a crooked smile and in English said, "See you later, alligator."

It was as if I'd been struck dumb. I knew there was something I was supposed to say in response, but hearing a "vicious killer" at Guantanamo Bay say "See you later, alligator" proved too much and I couldn't think of it.

After waiting through two beats of my befuddlement, Jaber almost nailed the punch line, "After a while, crocodile."

I must have had a dazed grin on my face when I found Stewart Aaron, the colleague who had been meeting with another client. Stewart was a partner and the first person I went to after I'd been asked if the firm would represent detainees. He and I had talked politics enough that I knew he would be sympathetic to the cause and, at least from my junior perspective, he wielded influence within the firm. Stewart had quickly gotten approval for us to take the case.

Stewart was standing with two lawyers from a different firm who also were on their first trip to Guantanamo. We followed a guard through the sally port (a secured area enclosed by two gates, which are never open at the same time) to Camp Echo's main entrance.

Our escort, a stocky marine gunnery sergeant who went by Gunny, was waiting for us. The Guantanamo Bay Naval Station is divided into Windward and Leeward sides. The Windward side was where the action was—and where the detention camps were; the much smaller Leeward side was where our lodging and the airport were. It was Gunny's charge to be with us at all times when we were on the Windward side of the base, unless we were in client meetings. Never having been a sailor, it was several days before I could figure out which side I was on.

Gunny belied a conspiracy theorist's notion that the military was trying to undermine our work. In fact, Baher Azmy, a law school professor and one of the few habeas lawyers who had gotten to the base before us, told me Gunny was the person to talk to about any issues, which proved to be true. Gunny was friendly, called operations people to make sure clients were ready for meetings, was willing to adjust his schedule when we asked, and even let us use the public library to get on the internet, which was hard to find on the base at that time. Admittedly this latter indulgence didn't seem like all that much until a subsequent trip when we were banned from entering the library, for reasons unexplained.

Even though Gunny was great, it struck me as overkill that we—US citizens with security clearances—had to be escorted at all times. That was especially so because there were hundreds of "third-country nationals"—or TCNs, as the military lovingly called them—from the Philippines, Jamaica, and Haiti wandering around the base. The TCNs were hired by private contractors to pave roads, drive ferries, bag groceries at the supermarket, and do the rest of the base's dirty work, often for subminimum wages. They didn't have security clearances but were everywhere, including at the detention camps, where they did construction work. I was glad they had freedom of movement, but I couldn't think of a legitimate national-security reason as to why they could wander around the grocery store unescorted, but we couldn't.

Our group piled into Gunny's Econoline van. He drove us away from the maze of detention camps and through a checkpoint. Within a couple of miles, we were passing what looked like suburban Phoenix, Arizona, complete with ranch houses, a golf course, and a high school. Having spent time on military bases in the Balkans, I had expected Guantanamo to be more, well, militarized. Instead, it was hard to imagine that shots had ever been fired in anger here, except maybe from a kid's BB gun.

We passed the base's commercial strip, featuring a McDonald's, a Subway sandwich shop, and a Navy Exchange supermarket (or NEX, as it was called), and pulled up at the cafeteria, which everyone called a galley since it was a naval base. There, you could eat as much lunch as you wanted for about two dollars. We sat together, below one of many TVs tuned to Fox News, and made small talk. When Gunny got up for more food, Stewart and I exchanged quick impressions.

"Jaber's really friendly, and he's got a good sense of humor. I think he'll be pretty easy to work with."

"My guy hardly said anything," Stewart reported. "He thought I was an interrogator."

Back at Camp Echo after lunch, I met with another client and realized that Jaber was going to be the exception, not the rule. This next client was far more reticent and suspicious, not that I could fault him. I found myself engaging in a series of monologues, trying to draw him out. Complicating things, Karim had gone with Stewart to another meeting because we had been told that my client spoke excellent English, which he didn't.

Just as we were developing some rapport, gun shots rang out, making us jump. Were they firing at detainees? There were too many shots for that (unless a bunch of guards had gone berserk), and I hadn't seen anyone in the camp carrying a gun. After a minute or so, I decided it must be target practice. I had seen live-fire exercises in Kosovo that followed a similar rhythm. The other possibility—that after forty-five years, Fidel Castro had picked this day to attack the Americans—was a tad unlikely. We had to shout for the rest of our meeting, and it was hard not to question why someone had decided to shoot what sounded like .50 caliber guns right then.

At 5:30, all of us got into Gunny's van outside Camp Echo. The lawyers passed their interview notes to him and, ceremoniously, he put them in a Kevlar bag with a small lock. He said they would stay in a safe for the night.

By the time we parked at the NEX alongside McDonald's, Camp Echo seemed far away. I felt exhausted as I watched families load groceries into minivans and buy Big Macs. It had made me more than a little stir-crazy to sit for hours in those tiny rooms, especially during the afternoon session. The idea of getting on the boat that would bring us to the Leeward side sounded great. I wanted to take a run or watch some mindless TV.

Immediately I felt kind of pathetic. Did I really think it had been a tough day because I'd spent a few hours in the detention camps? Jaber had spent every day and night there for several years and would be spending that night alone in a tiny cell. He had no idea if he would ever spend a night outside a cell again.

Gunny asked if we wanted to have dinner. He said there was a good Cuban restaurant on the base. The irony was intriguing, and we had wanted to buy Gunny a meal to thank him for his help. Also, the Leeward side galley—the only dinner option on that side—closed at 6:30 and we would have barely made it in time. "Cuban sounds good," someone said.

The Cuban place was built, evidently, to evoke a romantic Caribbean seaside shanty, complete with white Christmas lights and a mock thatch roof. We ordered from a menu that looked more Mexican than Cuban, and everyone got a beer. Maybe because I was the youngest of the group, Gunny picked me to complain to, albeit good-naturedly, that there were few attractive women on the base.

After my parents' divorce, my mom had a beat-up Datsun station wagon, complete with a hole in the floor and a plastic sheet where the tailgate door should have been. The rear bumper was intact, though, and my mom adorned it with a bumper sticker saying, "A woman without a man is like a fish without a bicycle." My seven-year-old brain struggled to make sense of that, but it was part of being taught not to objectify women. Still, I could see Gunny's point. I did my best to commiserate while working through a burrito. During dessert, Gunny nudged me and indicated with his eyes that I should look toward the door. One of the few attractive women had turned up.

"Not bad," I managed.

It was 9:00 p.m. when we got back to the Combined Bachelor's Quarters, or CBQ, as our accommodations were called. It was a cross between a Motel 6 and a college dorm, and might have been worth a complaint had we not spent the day with clients in their third year of indefinite detention. Stewart and I found Mark Sullivan, another colleague, who had flown down to Guantanamo that evening. With six clients, we wanted to have three lawyers conducting interviews, but Mark hadn't been able to make our flight the day before. Mark was a former prosecutor and experienced trial lawyer. He also had an enviably level-headed approach to things.

The three of us walked away from the CBQ and onto a dirt road that was flanked by fields of scrub brush. In the distance to one side was a marine barracks and a five-story building that housed TCNs (the acronym had lodged itself in my mind). To the other side, we could see a few guard towers and the hills that led to Cuba proper, outlined against the night sky. At the foot of the winding dirt road sat a beach we had yet to visit. From our vantage point, we had a beautiful view of the moon shining on the Caribbean, but enjoying it didn't feel right.

We wanted to debrief and, although none of us was ready to say our rooms were bugged, we felt safer discussing clients outdoors.

Also, because every word our clients had uttered to us was classified, we had to make sure that nobody heard us inadvertently.

"It's the cone of silence," Stewart joked.

Stewart told Mark, as he had told me, that his first client had pegged him for an interrogator and wouldn't talk. The second client had chatted a bit but had been far from forthcoming. When drawing up our meeting schedule for the military, I gave myself the two clients against whom the most extensive allegations had been made. Given that I had brought the case to the firm, it seemed only fair for me to take the more complicated clients. Ironically, Jaber had been by far the easiest client to deal with. Silently I thanked him. Stewart and I told Mark not to have any preconceptions, or at least not favorable ones, about how his people might greet him the next day.

When we got back to the CBQ, I was exhausted physically, but my mind was racing. I was thinking about the day and what Jaber was doing alone in his cell at Camp Echo that night. It was too late, and I was too full to take a run, so I watched a preview of the Red Sox–Cardinals World Series, hoping to distract myself. As a Yankees fan, I found it more pain than distraction. The only other viable option on TV was *A Few Good Men*, but I didn't need any reminders of Guantanamo, especially not the likes of Colonel Nathan R. Jessup.

At 11:30 p.m., I grabbed the Ambien that I normally saved for red-eye flights and took half a pill. Two sleepless hours later, I swallowed the other half and finally drifted off.

After what felt like five minutes, my alarm was buzzing. By 6:40 a.m., we were on the bus, heading to the 7:00 a.m. ferry that would take us across the bay to the Windward side. We had seen accommodations on the Windward side that would have saved us the hour-long commute to Camp Echo, but we weren't allowed to use them. Maybe the military just wanted us to enjoy the view from the ferry.

We reached Camp Echo at 8:00 a.m. Even though it had solitary confinement cells, Camp Echo didn't look like a world-class prison from the outside. We learned later that it wasn't used to detain large numbers of people for the long term. It had a temporary feel, in stark contrast to the cement-and-steel facility that sat across the street. That building, as a sign said, was Camp 5, where Jaber was normally held.

At the main entrance to Camp Echo, Gunny spoke into an intercom: "Habeas on the gate."

I had heard this phrase the day before but hadn't given it much thought. Now I grasped the meaning. We had filed habeas corpus petitions for our clients, so we were "habeas." It sounded strange, but they could have thought of something worse to call us. A guard came, checked IDs, and opened the gate.

Two other guards gave us a cursory pat down. Only a couple of lawyers had made the trip before us, and some of the procedures—like the search—seemed a bit ad hoc. They wouldn't stay that way for long.

We passed through the sally port and into the main area of Camp Echo, the gravel making a now-familiar crunching sound under our feet. Walking toward a building that had been designated as an attorney waiting room complete with a cell, we passed an enclosed metal mesh cage in the middle of the compound that might have been eight feet high and fifteen feet square. It had been deserted the day before. Now a detainee was trying to exercise by running around the cage as fast as he could. The problem was that he had to make a hard right turn about every three steps. It looked maddening. He glanced up for a second and caught my eye. I looked away.

A few minutes later, Karim and I walked into Jaber's room. I chuckled to myself that just twenty-four hours earlier I had paused in this same spot, worrying about being alone with a violent jihadist. Jaber smiled broadly and shook our hands.

I almost said, "How was your night?" before realizing how stupid that would sound.

"How bad was your night?" I asked instead.

Jaber smiled, suggesting an appreciation for my choice of words. "I was okay. How was your night?"

I wondered if there was an appropriate answer. If I said good, wouldn't that just make Jaber feel worse about his isolation? If I said bad, wouldn't I seem like a self-centered ingrate?

"It would have been better if you'd been with us."

I put some food on the table, including candy bars Jaber had requested. We chatted about nothing in particular while eating. Making small talk had quickly become easy. Jaber had just rebuffed my attempt to have him eat an apple when he said, "I want to tell you my story."

I had not expected this and reached immediately for a legal pad.

"I was trying to get home from Afghanistan. I went to a checkpoint on the border with Pakistan and asked to be taken to the Bahraini embassy. The Pakistanis laughed and took me with other Arabs to a prison."

"Jaber, I'm sorry to interrupt, but later I would like to talk about what happened when you were in Afghanistan."

"We will.

"I was in the Pakistani prison for sixteen days. They served food in a bucket, and the bread was inedible. I had shackles on my legs. They were not connected to each other with a chain like here, but with a steel bar. It was very painful.

"I was interrogated by the Pakistanis many times. There were no beatings, but there were threats. In the last few days there, two American men questioned me. One of them spoke Arabic fluently, but not as a native speaker. They did not use violence, but they did use abusive language. One cursed at me.

"On our last day in that prison, the Pakistanis put us in blue uniforms, handcuffed us, and made us wear blindfolds. We were taken to a military airport, where there was a plane with an American flag."

"How did you see the plane if you had a blindfold on?" I asked.

"The blindfold was not very good. You could see through it. And they took it off to put sacks over our heads.

"They shackled us to the floor of the plane with chains around our thighs, waists, and shoulders. The chains were pulled so tight, they pushed us forward. It was very painful to my stomach. I had surgery on my stomach six years ago because I was obese. I weighed about 115 kilograms."

It was almost impossible to picture Jaber at 250 pounds. I wanted more details about the surgery, but I decided I should stop interrupting. Karim continued interpreting.

"There are tubes in my stomach now, and I tried to tell a soldier that the chains were hurting me. He hit me in the stomach, and I vomited blood. After a couple hours of flying, they took us off the plane in Kandahar." I had read that Kandahar was a city in Afghanistan where the US had an airbase.

"The soldiers at the American base put everyone on the ground. We were connected to each other by a wire that was around our arms."

I glanced up from my notes and saw that Jaber had pulled himself away from the table—away from us. He wasn't looking in our direction anymore either, but off to the side of the room.

"The soldiers were walking on people. It felt like someone urinated on me. They beat people. One of them hit my head on the ground. Someone put his boot in my mouth. This went on for over an hour."

Jaber's voice had become quieter, as had Karim's.

"We were taken to a tent that had barbed wire around it, but no sides. It was open to the elements, and Afghanistan in winter is very cold. The soldiers continued to hit people. If you screamed, there was more beating.

"I was taken somewhere else, where there were lots of soldiers and a translator. I think he was Lebanese. He cursed at me and called me 'Al Qaeda, terrorist, dog.' They tore my clothes off and put their fingers in my anus. They took photographs of me.

"The next morning, they took me for an interrogation. They made me walk barefoot on barbed wire to get there. They hit my head against a metal hangar and said it was an accident. They pushed me to the ground, where there was broken glass."

Jaber pointed to a scar on his knee and looked in my direction. "This is from the glass." He looked away again.

"The interrogator was Black. I told him I would sign anything, and there was no need to beat me. He said that beatings were not allowed and left. Another soldier called me a terrorist and poured hot liquid on me. I said I needed a doctor. The soldier spit on me and said, 'We brought you here to kill you.'

"A soldier put a cigarette out on me," Jaber said, pointing to a small circular scar on his wrist. "The soldier said that he did it in the name of God and Christ.

"We had MREs"—Jaber used the English acronym for meals ready-to-eat—"in the morning and at night, or sometimes just one time a day. We were often dizzy from hunger. We told the Red Cross, and they began to bring us Afghan bread. We were supposed to get one piece, but the guards only gave us half. When I told the Red Cross about this, we started getting a quarter of a piece.

"For a bathroom in the tent we used a bucket, which was full of feces. I saw a soldier put a Qu'ran into the bucket. Another time, I saw a soldier search the Qu'ran with his boots.

"I was in Kandahar for two weeks. I could never sleep because of the hunger and cold. One night, they took me to another tent with my hands and legs tied and a sack on my head. They plucked some of the hairs of my beard and they shaved my moustache. They used scissors to cut off my clothes and took me to a different tent with other naked detainees. They put us in orange clothes and tied us with chains. I had to crouch for hours with my hands tied in front of me. It was very cold."

Jaber's words came more slowly now, but in an unrelenting rhythm.

"At eleven o'clock, they put very tight goggles on me that I could not see through. They placed something on my ears so I could not hear. They took us to an airplane and chained us to the floor. I said that the chains made my stomach hurt. Beating was the response. When they saw that I was in great pain, they brought me sleeping pills.

"Somewhere, after many hours, they dragged us off the plane as if we were little boxes. They put us on a second plane. It seemed we were on that second plane for a whole day. The goggles were so tight that they made my nose bleed. They gave me more sleeping pills.

"When we arrived in Cuba, they tied us together on the ground for many hours. They took me to a concrete building in which they took off my clothes and took photographs of me. They gave me a very cold shower and very tight clothes.

"They took me to Camp X-Ray."

Camp X-Ray, I knew, was the original detention facility at Guantanamo, which had been built in a matter of weeks. I had seen photographs showing that it consisted of a series of open-air cages, like a kennel.

"We were forbidden to move. We had to sit still. If you even turned around in your cage to look at someone, there would be a punishment. Sometimes we were forbidden to pray. Later, they allowed us to pray, but not to face Mecca. Then we were allowed to face Mecca. But whenever there were new detainees, we were again prohibited from looking at each other or praying.

"We had rats, snakes, and scorpions in the cages, but no bathrooms. When we left the cages to use the bathroom, they always chained us and pushed our heads down hard. It was too painful, and the chains caused injury. When we refused to get chained to go to the bathroom, they gave us buckets to use in the cell.

"I was in X-Ray for three months. At the end, I tried to kill myself by breaking a metal piece from my cell and swallowing it. I was in the hospital for three days."

Jaber put his elbows on his thighs and his face in his hands. He pulled back even more from the table, although the shackles kept him from going far.

"When I came back from the hospital, the head of shift took everything out of my cage. He pushed me to the floor and cursed me. I yelled at him, and he told the staff sergeant to get the IRF." Jaber pronounced "IRF" as if he were saying it in English.

I knew "IRF" was shorthand for Immediate Response Force, a team of five soldiers, wearing helmets, face masks, chest protectors, and shin guards, tasked—supposedly—with subduing unruly detainees. I had seen some of this equipment in the Camp Echo bathroom that morning.

"A lieutenant came and told me to get on the ground. I went down and put my hands on my back. I saw the IRF coming, and it had six people instead of five." Jaber started to cry softly.

"The staff sergeant opened the door and a very big guard, wearing all his gear, ran in. He jumped in the air and landed on my back. He held my neck, and two others held my legs. A female guard hit my head on the floor repeatedly. The staff sergeant said, 'Don't leave until he bleeds.' The guard kept choking me, and I thought I was going to die. Blood gushed out of my nose, and I lost consciousness. Other detainees told me later that the female guard held my face up for the camera."

I had read that all IRF interventions were videotaped.

"I woke up in the naval hospital, the one that they use for the military, not for detainees. I saw the same staff sergeant holding a video camera. They gave me an IV and a CAT scan. While I was in the hospital, a female interpreter, who said that her name was Alin, came and asked me about the incident. It was the first beating like that. Everyone knew about it."

Without making eye contact, Jaber raised his head and pointed to a scar on his nose. "I have this from the beating."

He buried his face again in his hands, choking back tears. Karim was ashen and looking down. His eyes were wet.

A month earlier, I had read a report by former British detainees who were back in the UK. They had seen Jaber's beating and described it in equally graphic terms. They wrote that after Jaber was pulled from his cell, guards came to clean the cell with a hose. The water turned red from his spilled blood. I had been expecting this story, but hearing it gave me chills.

I let a moment or two pass, wanting to be sure that Jaber had finished. He kept his face in his hands and didn't say a word. There were no tissues, so I put a few napkins in front of Jaber, not that he could see them.

"I am so sorry to hear about what you experienced," I said softly, as Karim translated.

"I cannot imagine how painful that must have been. I cannot imagine how painful it is now. No human being should have to endure those things. I don't know if you've ever been able to tell those stories to anyone who cared. I want you to know that we care."

I paused. Jaber didn't move.

"We will do everything we can to make sure those kinds of things never happen again. I promise. You are not alone in that way anymore." I didn't know if there was anything we could really do.

Jaber didn't respond. We sat in complete silence for a minute.

"I am so sorry. Nobody should ever be subjected to that kind of abuse." I was repeating myself, but I hoped it might help Jaber absorb my words. He still hadn't looked up. I thought about moving around the table to put my hand on his shoulder, but I wasn't sure if it was appropriate.

Karim leaned over and whispered, "May I speak to Jaber in Arabic?"

I nodded. Karim spoke in words I didn't understand, but with an unmistakably gentle tone. Jaber remained silent and motionless.

I worried that revisiting the trauma Jaber had experienced would overwhelm him. He had already tried to kill himself. He would be spending the rest of that day and the night alone in his cell. For the first time—but certainly not the last—I wondered if Jaber would be better served by a therapist than an attorney.

"Jaber, I would like to ask you some questions. I just want to make sure that I understand everything you've told us. Is that okay?" I asked quietly.

I hoped to bring him back to the present without making it appear I was ignoring what he had said. The lawyer in me also knew that I needed more details.

But there was something else at work, even though I had trouble admitting it. I don't trust people easily, especially when I don't know them. To me, there's nothing worse than getting suckered into believing in someone who later takes advantage of that trust. I guard against that, at some level, most of the time. It's an approach that probably helps me as a lawyer, but people I'm close to don't always appreciate my vigilance.

Here, how could I know for sure what was going on? There had been conviction behind each of Jaber's words. His pain and horror had taken on a palpable presence in the room as tangible as his shackles. And I had developed an affection for him in a short time.

But what did I really know about him after one day? How could I know if he was or wasn't some kind of bad guy? Was he telling me the truth or just using me to spread anti-American propaganda?

I felt it was right, as a human being, to be purely compassionate in that moment. It also was the right thing to do as an attorney who was trying to develop a relationship with a new client under the worst conditions. Still, I could feel my doubts lurking in the background.

Jaber looked up and wiped his eyes. "We can talk about your questions."

"Thank you. I can only imagine how difficult this must be. I just want to make sure that I understand everything that happened."

He nodded.

"Do you know the name of the head of shift who called for the IRF?" The report by the British detainees had named some of the guards who had participated in the beating, but I wanted to see if Jaber knew any of them himself.

"Collins," he said, very quietly.[1]

"How do you know his name? The guards I've seen have their name tags covered." In fact, there was a sign outside Camp Echo warning staff to "sanitize" their uniforms.

"Before, we could see their names."

"Do you know the name of the staff sergeant?"

"Williams."

---

1 The names of the people who took part in the IRF beating were disclosed in the British detainees' report. Further, my interview notes, containing those names, were deemed unclassified. Nonetheless, Guantanamo authorities often have talked about the possibility that detention camp staff could be harmed if their identities become known. Without commenting on the merits of that notion, I have used pseudonyms here.

"How about the female guard who hit your head?" I kept my voice as quiet and calm as I could.

"She was Thomas."

"You talked about the large guard who came into your cell first. Do you know his name?"

"Sanders. Later, I asked him why he had jumped on me. He said, 'Because I'm Christian.'"

"God,"—I didn't mean it as any kind of pun—"what an asshole." I stayed quiet for a moment, and so did Jaber.

"You said that Williams told the IRF, 'Don't leave until he bleeds.' I assume he said that in English. How did you understand what he said?"

"I am able to speak some English, and I could hear that he said something like that." I wasn't entirely surprised. At times, Jaber seemed to laugh at my jokes, weak as they were, before Karim translated them completely.

"Is your English good enough that we could talk without translation?"

"It has gotten better since I've been here, but I am not always that comfortable with it."

"I understand. Did you talk to anyone other than Alin, the translator, about the incident?"

"I talked to a man who said he was from the FBI."

"What did you tell him?"

"I told him what I have just told you."

"When did that conversation take place?"

"Not long after the incident."

"What was his reaction?"

"He was surprised. He said that he would investigate."

"Did you ever see him again?"

"No."

"Do you know if Alin ever did anything about the incident?"

"Nothing I know of."

I looked through my notes for other questions: How did you know that you were in Kandahar when you got off the plane there?

Did you ever sign a statement in Kandahar after you said you would? What did you mean that you and the other detainees were connected by "wire" that was around your wrists in Kandahar? Do you know what date you arrived in Cuba? Where did you have the surgery on your stomach?

As Jaber answered, his voice became stronger. He started looking me in the eye again. I nibbled on a biscuit, hoping he might follow suit. He did, although not with the same gusto as before.

Jaber said the surgery had been performed at a hospital in Jeddah, Saudi Arabia.

"I have to say, it's really hard to imagine you overweight, Jaber." He was now little more than a gaunt specter.

"I was fat," he said, his expression easing somewhat.

"Amazing. Does that mean I should only bring healthy food here?"

"I am on the Guantanamo diet now. You have to bring good things."

"Okay, I promise."

"Tomorrow, can you bring me a McDonald's Filet-O-Fish with extra mayonnaise?"

"Sure. Is that really what you want?" It's not as if there were a gourmet shop on the base, so I didn't have much to offer, but it still wasn't what I would have expected.

"And a Sprite, please."

"You got it."

It was nearly noon, and we had to leave. I was concerned about how Jaber would manage alone in his cell. I told him at least three times that we would be back the next day. He nodded, looking distracted and sad.

In a now familiar ritual, guards knocked loudly on the door. I gathered my things. Karim and I both gave Jaber little hugs.

"Was that a large or small Sprite you ordered, sir?" I asked.

"Large," Jaber said, almost smiling.

"We'll see you tomorrow."

Guards surrounded Jaber, shackling his hands. He looked very small.

I was thinking about the IRF incident as we walked into the hot Cuban sun. It seemed like the gravel under our feet radiated heat. I felt beads of sweat forming under my short-sleeved button-down shirt almost immediately.

In some ways, the IRF beating was the easiest thing to get my head around. We had the report by the British detainees and Jaber's scar. Jaber's account was internally consistent and consistent with that of the Brits. I also knew that the Bahraini government had made an official inquiry to the US about the incident. I was as sure as I could be that retelling the story had made Jaber genuinely anguished.

In my gut, I started to believe Jaber had been on the receiving end of a serious beating. As bad as it is to be suckered, I've always had a visceral reaction to bullies. It's an impulse that had gotten me in trouble at times, including as a young kid who just couldn't walk away when a bigger kid was picking on someone. I got myself punched in the face more than once. Obviously a six-person IRF team against an unarmed 140-pound man is not a fair fight.

As we waited to leave Camp Echo, I wondered whether we might be able to track down the sergeant and the guards who had been involved and sue the crap out of them.

I had been in Guantanamo for two days. It felt like a year.

Chapter 2

BACK IN THE FIGHT

It was exhausting and demoralizing to be at Guantanamo. Truth be told, I also was exhilarated. In the two years that I had been at the New York firm since returning from my second stint in Kosovo, commercial litigation had made me fairly miserable. It wasn't that I had moral qualms about work that mostly involved well-funded entities fighting over money, but representing financial services companies or banks was uninspiring to say the least. It never really mattered who won or lost—although I much preferred winning—because it was just a question of moving dollars from one place to another.

It wasn't anything like Kosovo. For those not obsessed with a region that has shrunk from view in recent years—and to sum up one thousand years of history—Kosovo was an area in Serbia, the largest republic of the Socialist Federal Republic of Yugoslavia. As Serbs told it, Kosovo had been an integral part of Serbia since medieval times, except for about five hundred years of Ottoman rule (which we can ignore for present purposes).

By the mid-1990s, the Socialist Federal Republic of Yugoslavia had dissolved following the secession of the republics of Croatia,

Slovenia, Bosnia, and Macedonia, which led to vicious wars. The Socialist Federal Republic of Yugoslavia then rechristened itself as the Federal Republic of Yugoslavia (FRY), which consisted only of Serbia and tiny Montenegro.

At that point, the population in Kosovo was perhaps 90 percent ethnic Albanian, nominally Muslim, and increasingly suffering oppression from Serbian and FRY authorities. By 1998 and 1999, a rebellion in Kosovo saw Serbian/FRY military and paramilitary forces engage in a deadly campaign against the Albanian population in Kosovo. The US spearheaded a seventy-eight-day NATO bombardment in the spring and summer of 1999 that led to the withdrawal of those military and paramilitary forces, to be replaced militarily by a NATO force called KFOR and a UN-led civil administration.

I had first gone to Kosovo at that point in 1999, almost on a whim. I was studying for the bar after finishing law school and had a job lined up at a large Seattle law firm. I told the firm that I wanted a few months off after the bar and, to my surprise, they agreed. I was trying to decide whether to spend my time stretched out on a beach or somewhere in Italy perhaps, when I read an article in the *New York Times* reporting on the aftermath of the NATO campaign in Kosovo.

I decided to go there to try to help. I don't know why that thought came to me. I had never done humanitarian aid work. But once I had the thought, I knew I had to do it. It was like love at first sight. You can't necessarily explain why you feel such a pull to a person, but you know you're going to act on it.

I tracked down Jordan Dey, a friend who was working with Kosovar refugees in Albania for Relief International, a fledgling aid group. Jordan was heading into Kosovo shortly. About a month later I was on a UN World Food Programme flight from Albania to Kosovo to be a Relief International volunteer, terrified that I had bitten off more than I could chew.

I spent the next few months based in western Kosovo. It turned out to be the most dramatic experience of my life to that point.

I handled logistics for an emergency shelter project that aimed to put one warm, dry room into war-damaged homes so that families could survive the brutal Balkan winter. That required me to run around Kosovo, Montenegro, and Macedonia buying lumber, nails, wood-burning stoves, and doors. Considering that my only prior construction experience had been on a monthlong sewer lagoon project after college, the learning curve was steep. Once I made deals for materials, I saw that the right stuff was shipped out to our construction crews made up of former soldiers of the Kosovo Liberation Army, a guerilla force that had fought Serbia/FRY. There was no ambivalence to the work. There was no ambiguity. People had been burned out of their homes and would die if they didn't have somewhere to stay. I wouldn't have traded a day of my time there for anything.

Returning to the States in November 1999, I got a fever within two hours of walking into my law firm in Seattle, perhaps the most obviously psychosomatic reaction on record. I spent the next week at home on the couch and the next year scheming to get back to Kosovo. In early 2001 I did, this time as a lawyer. For the next year and a half, I worked on criminal cases involving international law and spent a lot of time in diplomatic negotiations for the release of detainees, perhaps a harbinger of what was to come.

In mid-2002, I left Kosovo after that second stint, partly because I wanted to burnish my domestic legal credentials and get some hardcore legal practice experience. A good number of people in the "international community" (to use a stock phrase for people working abroad with the UN or aid groups) are middle-aged and don't seem qualified to be employed other than in international mission environments. In my experience, many of those people have families at home. While missions are great, I was concerned about ending up as an older international community refugee who had few options for a more stable domestic-side life, given that I had only practiced in the States for about a year. So, I decided to head back to New York and work for a firm to get real nuts-and-bolts legal training. I hoped it would be good for me from a long-term perspective, even if I knew it would lack for excitement at times. But what a lack it turned out to be.

Here at Guantanamo, I was at least back in the fight. Having established a relationship with Jaber during our first two sessions, I needed to address the accusations the government had made against him. I spent the night before our third meeting studying those accusations, which had been generated by a Combatant Status Review Tribunal (CSRT). The CSRTs were ad hoc proceedings instituted nine days after the Supreme Court had ruled in June 2004 that the detainees could bring court cases. In theory, the CSRTs were implemented to determine if the detainees were "enemy combatants." In truth, these tribunals were a satirist's idea of due process. Detainees did not have lawyers or access to classified evidence, which could be the only form of evidence against them. They were invited to present their own evidence, but nobody explained how someone being held incommunicado in Cuba was supposed to gather inculpatory materials from thousands of miles away. Despite being a farce, the CSRTs produced the only allegations against our clients.

The CSRT accused Jaber of things such as going to Bosnia to fight, being arrested in connection with a bombing in Saudi Arabia, and being at Tora Bora in Afghanistan. If you looked at the allegations closely, they asserted less than they initially suggested. But still, all of this was happening against the backdrop of 9/11, which had a tendency to make people view suspicions as fact.

Of course, it wasn't as if anyone had to tell me about the significance of 9/11. I was born and raised in New York. With a classic chauvinist's perspective, "New York" meant Manhattan to me, period. So, it was *my* city that had been attacked that day (obviously there were tragedies in DC and Pennsylvania as well). Not a day went by that I didn't think about 9/11 in one way or another. In fact, when I saw signs or other messages saying "Never forget" in relation to 9/11, I wondered how anyone possibly could.

Just before the attacks, in early September 2001, I had been in New York for a brief visit from Kosovo. Walking around downtown Manhattan with a friend, I pointed out that the Twin Towers were a great landmark if you were lost and wanted to figure out which way was downtown and which way was up. As I was getting ready to fly to the Balkans on September 3, I heard a lot of "Stay safe" and "Be careful," as I normally did when going back to Kosovo. The sentiments were appreciated, but I wasn't worried particularly about my safety, since I was very familiar with Kosovo by that point. I had no idea how justified I was in not being worried about myself as I left New York.

On September 11, I woke up thinking of my grandfather, Dom Colangelo. His birthday was September 11, 1911. He had passed away in the mid-1990s, but I always associated the day with him. After saying a few words to him in my mind, I headed to work.

A delegation from the FRY was going to be visiting that day. In theory, their mission was to advocate for Serb civilians who had stayed in Kosovo after Serb authorities withdrew. The Serbs still in Kosovo, particularly in areas that did not border Serbia, faced isolation, economic difficulties, and threats from Kosovar Albanians who wanted revenge. So, FRY officials were their self-appointed protectors. To put it more charitably, some of those officials were genuinely concerned for their compatriots. But some undoubtedly saw great political advantage in taking on the mantle of defender.

I had become something of an interlocutor between the UN administration in Kosovo and authorities in Serbia by that point, having already traveled to Belgrade to meet with a committee created to address issues relating to Serbs still living in Kosovo. That had been one of the first trips to Serbia by anyone working for the UN in Kosovo.

Politically I had little common ground with my Belgrade counterparts, whose public position at least was that the ethnic Albanians in Kosovo were basically all Islamic terrorists whose violent conduct warranted the brutal military response leveled at them by Serbia/FRY in 1998 and 1999. The narrative was that the West should have been grateful to Serbs for taking on these terrorists before they could attack others.

Anyone who knew about the wanton destruction of homes, the displacement of hundreds of thousands of refugees, and the killing of civilians in Kosovo couldn't swallow that narrative. And the idea that Albanian "terrorists" posed a legitimate threat to the US or other countries in Europe was silly. I had never met a more pro-American group of people than Kosovar Albanians—and that includes your average sampling of Americans in the good old USA.

Kosovar Albanians adorned their homes with photographs of Bill Clinton, Madeleine Albright, and General Wesley Clark, who headed the NATO campaign. They celebrated Senator Bob Dole, whose advocacy for them led some in Serbia to claim falsely he was Albanian.

Once, I was in the passenger seat of a car that backed into a late model BMW in a Kosovo parking lot, leaving a nasty dent. I got concerned when a tall, burly, track-suited, crew-cut-sporting man jumped out of the BMW. But when he found out we were Americans, he smiled and thanked us for American support. "Don't worry about the car," he said.

I gave him two hundred deutschmarks I kept hidden on me for emergencies, just to be fair and because he really did look like he could do damage. When I learned later that this gentleman was a bodyguard for Hashim Thaci, a politician and the former head of the Kosovo Liberation Army, it reinforced my sense that the money had been well spent.

Perhaps most tellingly, when I had been in Kosovo after the war in 1999, there were reports that Osama bin Laden had made threats against Americans there. The name was only passingly familiar at the time. But several former Kosovo Liberation Army soldiers had told me not to worry, saying in rough paraphrase, "If we see anyone who looks like bin Laden, we'll take care of him."

Even though the Belgrade contingent's official narratives about Kosovo were hard to stomach, I had formed passable working relationships with a number of those coming to Kosovo on September 11, and I was part of the UN group that would meet them. They arrived at our designated meeting spot on a quiet side road in an armored personnel carrier so massive that it almost looked comical, escorted by KFOR vehicles.

To be fair, this kind of security arrangement wasn't gratuitous. The hostility of Kosovar Albanians toward Serbs was palpable. Two years earlier, in 1999, I had been in Peja, a city in Kosovo's west. A convoy of cars driven by Serbs who were leaving Kosovo had mistakenly been routed through the city center by KFOR escorts. When the Kosovar Albanians in the city realized what was happening, they set upon the convoy with a visceral rage. It was only because squads of Italian soldiers formed a perimeter around the convoy and began fighting the crowd that the damage was not worse. The fury in the faces and voices of the crowd stayed with me. It made sense that a people whose homes had been destroyed and loved ones killed would hate the perpetrators, but among the women, children, and elderly cowering in their cars that day were many who were not direct—or indirect—perpetrators. The fury and rage had not dissipated in the two years since that incident.

In a few UN vehicles, we followed the KFOR column and the APC to Gračanica, a Serb-majority town about ten kilometers outside Pristina, the main city in Kosovo where we worked. Swedish members of KFOR efficiently guarded the main entrances to town as well as perimeter areas. After we passed through the checkpoint, we visited a Serbian Orthodox church monastery. The Belgrade delegation then met with residents. To say the UN was unpopular in Gračanica would be an understatement. Local Serbs had never wanted Belgrade to give up control of Kosovo, let alone to international overlords. The dirty looks we got from local toughs and old ladies alike just driving through town were withering, so our UN group decamped to a local restaurant we hoped was a more controlled environment. After a while, the Serbian mission joined us for lunch.

Pork was not served in Kosovar-Albanian communities because it was prohibited by Islam. Not many Albanians were practicing Muslims, as underscored by the ubiquity of short dresses and booze in Kosovo's larger towns and cities. However, some cultural aspects of Islam had lingered, like not eating pork, taking your shoes off in homes, and broadcasting the call to prayer from mosques (not that many answered). Serbian cuisine, by contrast, often features pork. Expats in Kosovo acted as if they had been given their first taste of food after weeks on a desert island when they had a pork meal, and there were enthusiastic comments from around the table about the pork ćevapi. Personally, the temporary absence of pork from my diet never seemed like a big deal, so instead of joining in that revelry, I talked with a lanky, bearded Serb named Vladimir about New York. He was doctrinaire, at least in official communication, but personable enough. And like so many people you meet around the world, he had an uncle in New York. He hoped to visit soon.

Around 2:00 p.m., the groups said goodbye and went to their vehicles. The Serbian crew was heading back to the FRY-Kosovo border—or boundary, as they called it. We headed to Pristina.

I was walking into our office a bit after 3:00 p.m. when I saw Tony Ricci, a colleague who several years later worked on Guantanamo issues for the Pentagon and the State Department. In his Boston accent, Tony said something about a plane hitting the World Trade Center. His light tone suggested he thought some bozo had flown a Cessna into the Twin Towers. I shook my head, wondering how anyone could be so stupid and recalling a story my grandmother told about a plane flying into the Empire State Building when she worked there in the 1940s.

Upstairs at my desk, I tapped my computer keyboard and tried to find out what had happened. The internet in Kosovo generally operated somewhere between slowly and not at all. I got nothing but that annoying circle just spinning on the screen. For a few moments I was distracted by a work issue, before a colleague said something about another plane hitting the Towers. That didn't make sense, obviously, but the internet was still out of commission. My colleague didn't know anything more but said he heard the news from someone who had been watching on TV at a restaurant down the street.

With growing anxiety and confusion, I walked to the restaurant. Clearly its satellite dish was working because a large crowd was quietly watching images of both Towers burning many floors up. There was no way this was some stupid accident.

Immediately I thought of my brother, Jeremy, and stepsister, Kate. Jeremy worked in New Jersey but lived in New York. Every morning he rode his bike to the Towers to get a PATH train to New Jersey. Typically he locked up his bike at about 8:30 a.m. I did some quick math to account for time zones. This whole thing must have started sometime close to 8:30 a.m. I knew Kate had started working at a restaurant near the World Trade Center, although I wasn't sure how close it was to the Towers themselves or when her shifts were.

A man in the crowd interrupted these thoughts, pronouncing loudly that the US should have expected this, given how it was throwing its weight around the world. Obviously he took this to be a coordinated attack. Criticizing American foreign policy is no doubt legitimate, but this was not the time—at all. With anger surging inside me, I was about to tell him that in a sentence that probably would have started with "Motherfucker . . ."

But then the South Tower collapsed. The blood rushed to my face and head as if I had been punched. Disoriented, verging on panic, thoughts of Jeremy and Kate ran through my mind in a jumble. Jeremy is a serious endurance athlete, the kind of person who looks just a tad winded after an Ironman triathlon. Even if he had been locking up his bike under the Towers at the worst possible moment, nobody could haul to safety faster than he could. I pictured him outsprinting people away from the Towers. I knew Kate was good at finding highly paid bar and restaurant gigs. She knew the money was in serving drinks, so it's not as if she would work breakfast, I told myself. But these hopeful thoughts vanished as I watched a massive plume of toxic debris spread down Manhattan streets at what looked like a hundred miles per hour, covering everyone who was there.

I desperately wanted to look away, but I also had a forlorn hope I might see my family or someone else I knew, so I made myself stare intently at the screen. Needless to say, I didn't recognize anyone. Realizing I was not going to find out anything about Jeremy and Kate watching TV, I stumbled back to the office.

I picked up the phone at my desk. Normally phone calls to the States worked reasonably well. Now, I couldn't even get a local dial tone on the UN system. I kept hanging up and trying again. Finally I did get a dial tone, but when I tried Jeremy's number, nothing happened. No delayed ring, nothing except silence. After that, I couldn't even get a dial tone.

I have no real memory of how, but I made my way to a friend's office in another building. He worked directly with the head of the UN administration, so I had the stress-induced idea that their phone and internet service might be better. Naturally it wasn't.

I sat at a desk in my friend's office, continually picking up the phone and hitting refresh on an internet that had gone dark. At some point I heard that the North Tower had collapsed. In a full panic now, I again tried to picture Jeremy dashing to safety in Tribeca or maybe even as far away from the Towers as Greenwich Village. I tried to picture Kate not even having gotten out of bed yet, maybe after working a late shift at the restaurant.

I remember very little about the next six hours. A few people who knew I was from New York offered words of comfort, but I don't recall their words. It was as if everything in the world was frozen in place and in complete tumult at the same time. There was no safe place for my mind to go, no matter how hard I tried to find one. I got up a few times to find a TV that might have news, before remembering it wouldn't have news about my family. So mostly I sat, poking at the internet and lifting the phone's receiver.

Somehow, at 8:04 p.m., the internet creaked to life and a message from my mom appeared after what must have been my thousandth time hitting refresh:

> I know you must be worried about Jeremy as he bikes to the WTC to go to work. Rod [my stepfather] reasoned that Jeremy has to be safe because he only goes to the ground floor or lower, and there were 20 minutes to evacuate people from

> the entire building, below the crash site, and there have been people on TV who got out from the 90th floor. So, although we can't get to Jem now, I left a message at his office, but lines to NY are full, I feel he's safe. Also, the crash was at 9:30, and that's probably late for him to have been there . . . I called last night at 10:45 and he was going into bed which probably means he had an early morning today. So breathe, we're with you, and I'll find a way to stay in touch.

I appreciated my mom expressing her general sense that Jeremy was safe, but it didn't reassure me. I've never put much stock in someone's *feeling* that things are okay. But I did like how Rod was thinking. That made sense, and I focused on his paraphrased words.

Three minutes later, after another hundred frantic hits to the refresh button, an email arrived with the subject "YOUR FAMILY IS SAFE." It was from my cousin Kristen, who wrote:

> I'm sure you've been hearing the horrible news about the attacks in NYC and Washington. . . . I just wanted you to know that Jeremy and Kate were both home when it happened and are fine, Jeri [my stepmother] and your Dad are OK as well. I just spoke with Jeri and she's talked to them. She said to please send their love to you. You can't get through via phone to anywhere in the New York right now, but you can call me if you want to talk.

I felt a physical sensation of relief as if every muscle in my body and every synapse in my brain unclenched. I sat there with my eyes closed, just feeling numb. A half hour later, I got a message from Kate:

> As far as we know everyone we know is OK. I guess phone lines are clogged. Keep trying to call,

> but if you can't get through know that at least the family's OK. I don't know what else to tell you. It's pretty hard to get info right now. It's like watching a movie, Josh—it doesn't seem real. Jeremy had a meeting scheduled for 10:00 at WTC and that's why he was still home.

So, my brother hadn't been at the Towers to lock up his bike at the normal time, which would have been minutes before the first plane hit, because he was going to be *in* the Towers an hour and a half later? If I hadn't been numb and known he was safe, that would have been entirely terrifying news. And although she didn't say it herself (maybe not wanting to alarm me more), I learned from an email my dad sent minutes later that Kate was supposed to be at her restaurant that morning:

> By now you have heard from Kristen that we are all safe . . . but stunned and in anguish for those who are lost and those who are left. It is frightening to think that Jeremy and Kate go to the World Trade Center every day. Today, Jeremy had a Manhattan meeting and was still at home. Kate was scheduled to be there an hour after the disaster. We are out of town. Roads into city are closed. I haven't been able to get thru to you by phone. We'll stay in touch.

So much for my theory that Kate wouldn't bother working breakfast. I said thanks to no one in particular that I had not known the details of Jeremy's and Kate's plans for that morning.

But the personal news coming through the wires was not all good. Kate wrote later that night about a friend of my stepbrother: "He worked on the 109th floor and there is no word. This is horrifying. Send your hopes in his direction." He didn't survive. Neither did someone I knew from high school, who had started working in the Towers the month before.

I might have slept an hour or two that night before getting up, starting the generator at my house (power was intermittent), and turning on the TV. German news channels were coming in best on the dish, so mostly I watched footage without understanding what was being said. Or it may have been that I understood exactly what was being said without knowing a word of German. I mean, what could you say other than recounting the horror?

The days that followed were marked by a form of depression I'd never felt before. Everything was hopeless, everything was ruined. I was entirely aware of my family's outrageously good fortune that day and reminded myself of it, but those thoughts didn't lift the black cloud for long.

I felt best being with people from New York, even if we mostly sat in stunned silence. But New York is a global place, so many colleagues from around the world had worked there—or had an uncle, a second cousin, or a long-lost friend who lived there. Many of them were very sweet in offering condolences. Luli Bashi was a young lawyer from Albania who spoke impeccable English and usually translated my conversations with the president of the Kosovo Supreme Court. One day he found me and said, "In my mind New York has always been the place I could go and find a way to make a life even if the rest of the world falls apart. I could go there and shine shoes or something and find my place." Not that many years later, he became Albania's foreign minister (and sent a few Albanian troops to be part of the "coalition" fighting the US war in Iraq).

My greatest comfort at the time, though, came when I managed to get the satellite dish working better and had access to news channels from the States. The New York (and Long Island) accents of firefighters being interviewed were reassuring in their familiarity, even as the New York City Fire Department counted a staggering 343 lost members. And I shudder to say it now, given his subsequent pernicious lunacy, but Rudy Giuliani's press conferences were a bit of a salve. It was probably when I had those visual connections to New York that I most wanted to be there. As overly melodramatic as it sounds, I wanted to be there to show that nobody could knockout New York—ever.

As I heard people in the UN talk about a mission that would follow an inevitable military campaign in Afghanistan, I also had an impulse to go there. In those days right after 9/11, it felt intensely gratifying to think about being where the US was going to kick the shit out of the Al Qaeda terrorists who were responsible for 9/11 and their troglodytic, women-hating protectors, the Taliban. Years later, I recognize that feeling as the hopelessly simplistic and optimistic machismo that ended up getting us into massive problems in Afghanistan and Iraq. But in September and October 2001, the idea of payback sounded great.

Chapter 3

SO, WHAT WERE YOU DOING?

As we ferried toward the Windward side for our third day of meetings, I looked again at the CSRT allegations against our clients, including Jaber. I had spent a lot of time thinking about how best to ask a question that boiled down to "What the hell were you doing (if anything) that got you locked up in Guantanamo?" Some habeas lawyers had said they didn't plan to make those inquiries at all. Clients would assume they were really government agents interrogating them, which would be the end of any discussion. But I thought there was an opening to talk to Jaber about these issues because he had supplied information to the government in response to the CSRT accusations, as shown in the CSRT documents. So, rather than press Jaber on whether he had done the things he was accused of, or anything else, I could at least start by asking about the answers he had given to the government already. And I figured that I could ask generally about what he had told interrogators over his years of captivity.

After some snacking and pleasantries, I pulled out the CSRT accusations. Jaber didn't indicate that he had any problem talking about them.

I noted for Jaber that the CSRT made a blanket assertion that he was an "enemy combatant," which meant "an individual who was part of or supporting the Taliban or Al Qaeda forces, or associated forces that are engaged in hostilities against the United States or its coalition partners." The conclusion that Jaber was an enemy combatant appeared to be based on various sub-allegations.

The first sub-allegation was that Jaber had gone to Afghanistan in 1989 to train on an AK-47 assault rifle. I'd done the math. I knew Jaber was sixteen in 1989. And I knew now that he had been an overweight kid. So, the idea that he was in Afghanistan as a teenager to train as a guerilla fighter was far-fetched. Also, we had been on the same side as the Saudis in Afghanistan during the 1980s, supporting fighters against the Soviet Union. As a result, even if the allegation were true, Jaber would not have been fighting against the US but rather for the same cause as the US.

When I asked, Jaber confirmed that, as the CSRT reflected, he had openly admitted to being in Afghanistan for what amounted to a long weekend in 1989. But he explained it was a Saudi-government-sponsored trip to celebrate the Saudi role in forcing the Soviets to withdraw. The Soviets had withdrawn in early 1989, before Jaber's visit. We chuckled a bit at the image of an obese sixteen-year-old Jaber facing down Soviet helicopters. Quietly I decided we could easily handle the 1989 Afghanistan trip if it ever came up in court or elsewhere. Confirming this, during a second internal Guantanamo proceeding held subsequently that was called an "Administrative Review Board," the presiding officer stated, "No negative conclusions will be drawn about you participating in any military actions against the Russians," not that Jaber had even seen a Russian in 1989.

The second sub-allegation was that Jaber had gone to Bosnia in 1995 "to participate in the jihad." I had thought about this in advance as well. In 1995, some expatriate Muslims had been in Bosnia fighting against Serbian forces on behalf of Bosnian Muslims. But the US itself had bombed Serbian positions there at that time to protect Bosnian Muslims. Again, even if Jaber had been in

Bosnia fighting, he would have been on the same side as the US. That couldn't make him an enemy combatant.

With a sheepish smile, Jaber said that, as the CSRT document reflected, he had gone to Bosnia not to fight but because he had heard he could find a blond Muslim woman to marry there. He admitted that this plan had not worked out. I knew from my time in the Balkans that Muslims who came from other countries to fight in Bosnia had married local women, although I wasn't sure of their hair color. I made a mental note that this allegation was not one that could legitimately be used against us.

Third, according to the military, Jaber had "stated that he traveled to Baku, Azerbaijan, in 1996, to join other Arabs and fight in Chechnya." Jaber confirmed that he had told the CSRT about traveling to Azerbaijan with a friend to see the country. According to Jaber, the other person then went to Chechnya, but Jaber did not. Jaber had no idea where the assertion that he had admitted going to Chechnya to fight came from. There was something about the vagueness and geography of all this that made me a bit uncomfortable. But it wasn't as if the government claimed it had some independent evidence that Jaber had gone to Chechnya to fight. It was relying on a supposedly voluntary statement from Jaber, who had no reason to say that. Also, the government didn't claim Jaber admitted to fighting or doing anything else in Chechnya. Once more, though, even if he had fought there, it would have been against the Russians, which doesn't make you an enemy combatant for Guantanamo purposes.

Fourth, it was claimed that Jaber had been detained in Saudi for questioning in connection with the 1996 Khobar Towers bombing. That bombing, in an eastern Saudi city not far from where Jaber lived, had killed and injured scores of US service people. Jaber confirmed that he had told the CSRT about being arrested and questioned, as had been many others in the area. However, he had been released with an apology. He also pointed out that the US had blamed a Shiite militant group for this attack. Al Qaeda and the Taliban are extremist Sunni groups that, at best, are contemptuous of Shia. Jaber was Sunni. So, even if you assumed just for the sake of argument that he was a bad guy, he wouldn't have been with the bad guys who carried out the Khobar Towers bombing, not that he was accused of that. As Jaber told the CSRT, "I'm not trying to defend Al Qaeda, they did other explosions. I just don't want this [bombing] confused with Al Qaeda."

Fifth, the government claimed Jaber had gotten a Bahraini passport after his Saudi passport was revoked. I knew from some research that the Bahraini government was quite amenable to giving passports to certain Saudis. The ruling family in Bahrain is Sunni, while the population in Bahrain is majority Shia. The Bahraini government had made a practice of oppressing the Shia majority in various ways, which allowed the minority Sunni population to hold power. In that context, the Bahraini government had sought to increase the ranks of Sunni citizens, including by granting citizenship to Sunni Saudis in certain tribes, like Jaber's. As such, nothing about Jaber getting a Bahraini passport was unusual. Jaber said he had told the CSRT that he held both passports, pointing out that delegations from both countries had visited him in Guantanamo. It is worth noting that these visits were often made by security officials from a detainee's home country and generally consisted of interrogations rather than tender, loving care. In any event, having two passports does not make one a terrorist.

Last, the government alleged that Jaber had gone to Afghanistan in 2001, had been "present at Tora Bora" (which is in Afghanistan), and had entered Pakistan from Afghanistan without proper documentation. Finally we were at the heart of things, at least in theory.

Jaber recounted his version of events as he had to the CSRT. According to Jaber, he had owed his former brother-in-law ten thousand Saudi riyal (amounting to a few thousand dollars). After divorcing Jaber's sister, the former brother-in-law threatened to have Jaber thrown in jail absent repayment, which evidently was a legal option in Saudi. Having few choices, Jaber spoke to a cleric he knew who was renowned for his philanthropy. Jaber asked for financial help. The cleric said he was sponsoring projects in Afghanistan to build mosques, but he was not sure how the projects had been progressing. The cleric had not heard from his Afghan contacts and could not find anyone to go to Afghanistan to check on the status of things because people feared an impending war there following 9/11. The cleric offered Jaber $5,000 to go to Afghanistan, from which Jaber had to pay for his travel. Jaber was apprehensive about going there but felt he had no choice.

Jaber traveled through Iran to the Afghan border where he was able to meet Mohammed Gul, a contact of the cleric. The two went into Afghanistan together and spent a couple of days traveling to various building sites where Jaber took pictures. Then the US bombing campaign began. Jaber sheltered in Gul's house for several days. At that point, Gul suggested that Jaber let him hold Jaber's passport, since Arabs were being targeted because Al Qaeda had brought the bombing upon Afghanistan. Jaber complied, thinking it was better not to carry documentary proof of being Arab.

After some time, Jaber decided he needed to try to escape the fighting, which was not abating. Gul escorted Jaber toward the Pakistani border on foot. Close to the border, Gul said he had mistakenly forgotten to bring Jaber's passport. Jaber did not necessarily believe this because a passport from a Gulf country was a valuable item in Afghanistan. But given the ever-increasing danger, Jaber did not want to take time to figure out what really was happening and, instead, continued to the border. Once there, he asked to talk to the Bahraini embassy. Border guards agreed but then detained him. Jaber said that during his time in Afghanistan, he had never been to Tora Bora.

It was a lot to take in, and one could argue his chronology had real holes in it. Why would someone go to Afghanistan other than to fight when a war with the US was on the horizon? *Well,* I thought, *people do that kind of thing to perform humanitarian aid work.* Some might think of them as heroes precisely because they went toward the danger. In Kosovo, I knew people who had worked not just in post-conflict environments like that but also in active conflict zones. So, going to a place soon likely to see combat (or leaving that place) cannot alone make anyone an enemy combatant.

Another issue that concerned the CSRT panel was that Jaber didn't have documentation to corroborate his account of going to monitor construction projections and could not say exactly where the mosques he visited were or where he stayed. Even putting aside that he had lost his camera and was locked up continents away from where any documentation might be found, the absence of documents was not surprising. I thought about my initial stint in Kosovo, doing relief work right after the war there. I had stayed in a house that had no official street address, unless you count "the house across from the lumberyard in Vitomirica." I didn't have receipts to show I was buying building materials because all transactions were in cash, and any scrap of paper you might have gotten with a purchase was not worth hanging on to. I didn't have records of phone calls I had made because, other than a satellite phone for emergencies, there were no phones. Also, I had worked with dozens of former Kosovo Liberation Army soldiers—that is, people who had fought for a guerrilla force just months earlier. All of that could sound suspicious to someone who was challenging me on what I had done there. But such suspicion would have been just that.

I tried to focus on the crux of the matter. Again, going to and from Afghanistan didn't make you a combatant. That left the allegation that Jaber "was present at Tora Bora." Although the CSRT said nothing more, I knew that Tora Bora was the scene of a battle in Afghanistan after which bin Laden had escaped into Pakistan when the Pentagon failed to put enough troops on the ground to contain him. Presumably that's what the CSRT was referring to and implying Jaber did something there. But were we supposed to just infer that Jaber had been up to no good? Guessing at what you're accused of is not how due process works. And if the US had some additional detail, why would it not have included that?

The final item to discuss was a newspaper article from the CSRT file. The CSRT didn't allege anything in connection with the article, but there it was. The article referred to Jaber having given a "fiery" sermon at a mosque near Buffalo, New York, sometime in early 2001, and having spent time with members of the congregation after that. This was during a trip to the States he had told me about. According to the article, a group of young men from that community had gone to a training camp in Afghanistan later, although that was before 9/11. Ultimately they were prosecuted in the US for providing material support to terrorists. In the article, relatives and attorneys of the young men claimed Jaber had laid a "guilt trip" on them for not being able to name Islam's prophets and by saying that Muslim women who were being raped in Bosnia needed protection. This induced the men to go to Afghanistan and made Jaber a "recruiter," they said.

Jaber had addressed the article at the CSRT hearing, saying he had given a sermon at the mosque mentioned, but he had not been trying to recruit anyone. He told the tribunal, "If I was Al Qaeda, would I go to New York and say these things? I didn't know these people, and I didn't know what they think. I didn't know anything about them. Why would anyone go to an open community in the United States and tell the people there to fight against the United States? This is simply not true."

What to make of all this? The allegations about Afghanistan in 1989, Bosnia in 1995, Azerbaijan in 1996, the Saudi arrest in 1996, and having two passports all seemed suspicious. I mean, it could have been a hard-bitten terrorist's itinerary. If I were a military officer tasked with justifying the detention of someone who'd already been held for years, this is the kind of thing I would have focused on to create smoke, if not fire.

Yet if you drilled down on the allegations themselves, none of them involved hostile action, let alone against the US. That was true even if you took the allegations at face value while ignoring everything Jaber said about them.

It was very hard to know what to think about the newspaper article. Obviously it was in the file, but the government did not even try to make an official accusation relating to those issues. It certainly wasn't like the government was shy about basing accusations on the thinnest of reeds, so it seemed telling that there were no recruiting-related allegations.

That left us with the "present at Tora Bora" language. The CSRT did not say when Jaber supposedly was there or with whom. It did not say that he did anything there. If we accepted the allegation as true, can having been present at a place, without doing something more, legitimately get you locked up as an "enemy combatant"? It wouldn't be a good legal argument. Even purely from a national security perspective, wouldn't you need something more than being "present" to think a person should be locked up forever? And that was if you ignored Jaber's saying he had never been there.

I decided I wouldn't reach any firm conclusions that day. I also knew that at some point soon, we were going to see what we had been told was classified evidence against all our clients. Maybe that evidence would clear up all issues of guilt and innocence. In that moment, it seemed best to move on to other topics.

During this third meeting and our final one the following day, we talked about additional abuses that had been inflicted upon Jaber. As he had before, he pulled away from the table and put his head in his hands. He said that during one interrogation, his questioner had draped Israeli and US flags around him, telling him that there was a holy war between Christians and Jews on the one hand, and Muslims on the other. He talked about being short-shackled (meaning one's ankles and wrists are shackled to a bolt in the floor) for hours. Interrogators had told him that if he admitted to being a low-level Al Qaeda fighter, he would be held for only a few years. If he insisted upon asserting his innocence, they said, he would spend fifty years at Guantanamo.

Jaber described several suicide attempts beyond the one he had already told me about, each more disturbing than the one before. Once, he convinced a guard to give him a razor to shave in the shower. Jaber cut open his arm and, before fainting, used his blood to write on the shower wall in Arabic, "I killed myself because of the brutality of my oppressors." He pointed to a large scar below his bicep, which he said resulted from that attempt. I again lamented that I wasn't a therapist. There was going to be some tricky psychological ground to cover with Jaber.

Jaber was convincing when he talked about these episodes. My gut told me to believe him, but I've always questioned the ultimate value of gut reactions in that kind of situation, and I've seen studies suggesting they aren't worth much. I struggled again to figure out whether I should believe what Jaber told me. He talked about being wrapped in the Israeli flag. Was that more about Middle Eastern politics than an actual interrogation technique? Was it physically possible to cut open your arm and, before passing out, write a sentence with your blood on a wall?

Amid discussing these terrible episodes, Jaber continued to display the ironic sense of humor that made me comfortable with him. When talking about how US forces detained any Arabs handed to them by Afghan warlords or Pakistani police, he broke sardonically into song: "Bad boys, bad boys, whatcha gonna do? Whatcha gonna do when they come for you?" It was the theme from *Cops.* He had never seen the show but had gotten an idea of what the song was about from an English detainee who taught it to him. He wasn't bad at carrying a tune.

Chapter 4

THE LITTLE OLD LADY IN SWITZERLAND

When I returned to New York, we had to contend with the government's motion to dismiss our case. Essentially the government was claiming the Supreme Court decision I had told Jaber about, called *Rasul v. Bush*, was substantively meaningless. In arguing *Rasul* in front of the Supreme Court, the government had contended that US courts had no jurisdiction over habeas challenges by Guantanamo detainees, "jurisdiction" meaning the authority of a court to hear a case. The government's argument was that the detainees were foreigners being held outside the US who therefore were beyond the reach of law.

In the June 2004 *Rasul* decision, the Supreme Court considered the realities of Guantanamo, which it described as a "base . . . compris[ing] 45 square miles of land and water" that the US occupies "pursuant to a 1903 Lease Agreement executed with the newly independent Republic of Cuba in the aftermath of the Spanish-American War." The Supreme Court found that the "United States exercises plenary and exclusive jurisdiction" over Guantanamo, given that

Cuba has no legal right (from our perspective) or practical means of disturbing US control there, even if the US is not the formal sovereign. On that basis, the Supreme Court found that US courts had jurisdiction over the habeas cases.

By way of context, the 2004 *Rasul* decision arose out of several cases that had been brought for fourteen detainees two years earlier. The lawyers who initiated those actions in 2002 included a few big-firm attorneys and a group of public interest lawyers. The big-firm attorneys were from Shearman & Sterling, which had been retained to represent the Kuwaitis at Guantanamo. Tom Wilner and Neil Koslowe were the senior lawyers on that team. Tom was a serious DC player who came naturally to moral outrage about people being held potentially forever without any due process. He also sported a great pair of cowboy boots for court arguments, not that I imagine he ever wrangled cattle. Neil seemed to know everything about every legal issue that did or even might come up, whether about procedure, the rules for getting security clearance, or a DC judge's predilections. Neil offered his analysis measuredly, which I appreciated as a much more junior lawyer.

Clive Stafford Smith and Joe Margulies were long-time death-penalty defense attorneys. Clive had the kind of English accent and charm that made you wish you'd been born in London. It was said that getting between Clive and a camera was a bad idea, which it was, considering how good Clive was in front of a camera. Among other things, he had a knack for employing satire to show the absurdity of the government's positions. At one point, absurd as it sounds, the military accused Clive and his colleague, Zach Katznelson, of smuggling Under Armour briefs and Speedo bathing suits to a client. In response, Clive pointed out that, given security protocols, he and Zach could only have done that by wearing the briefs and Speedos into the interview room, stripping down with their client, and trading garments, which he swore had not happened. As I understand, the military did not push the point.

Joe Margulies was remarkably sharp and empathic. He also had a preternatural ability to find the practical advantage in what appeared to me were purely negative developments. If a client's conditions at Guantanamo worsened, Joe found a way to use that for litigation purposes. If there was a bad court decision, that was an opportunity in the court of public opinion. Thinking creatively like that, you could almost always stay on the offensive. It wasn't a strategy I had considered much before meeting Joe, but ever since, I have tried to find those practical advantages. And there are clear psychological benefits to identifying alternative angles rather than just feeling lousy when things go south.

The original crew of Guantanamo lawyers also included Michael Ratner and Barbara Olshansky from the Center for Constitutional Rights. They had always been fearless in representing clients for reasons of principle, even if those clients were being vilified. And they didn't do it for the money—they worked at a small nonprofit. At times, you hear lawyers say they shouldn't be blamed for representing bad clients since everyone is entitled to a defense. But to me, if you represent people or businesses who have engaged in terrible conduct because it earns you hourly rates of four figures, that's entirely different from undertaking a case that will pay little to nothing simply because there is principle to vindicate.

I did my best to learn from this group, especially concerning the government's motion to dismiss all habeas petitions that we now had to oppose. In the government's motion, which was made to the DC district court where the habeas cases were pending, the government said *Rasul* only resolved a very narrow question. That question was whether US courts had jurisdiction to accept cases filed by the detainees, but not whether the detainees had any rights a US court could vindicate. Again, the government said that foreigners being held in Cuba as "enemy combatants" had no enforceable rights.

So, in the government's telling, *Rasul* had decided that detainees were allowed to file cases, but those cases had to be thrown out immediately because no detainee had a single cognizable right. Obviously it sounded to us that the government was recycling rejected arguments. It also seemed absurd to say the Supreme Court had gone through the trouble of deciding *Rasul* simply for the academic purpose of allowing habeas petitions to be filed even though no petition could state valid claims under any circumstances.

The government went on to argue that even if detainees were entitled to some due process, they had received it through the CSRTs, the procedures at Guantanamo that generated the allegations against Jaber and in which detainees had no lawyer or right to see evidence. Also, those proceedings were staffed by military officers who knew not only that the CSRTs were convened for the sole purpose of keeping courts from evaluating habeas petitions but also that the secretary of defense (not to mention the president and vice president) were on record talking about how evil all detainees were. It was difficult to imagine the stones it would take for an officer to vote to release a detainee under those circumstances.

The DC district court judges who had randomly been assigned to hear Guantanamo cases agreed (with one exception) that Joyce Hens Green, a retired judge, should handle the cases in a coordinated way, including to decide the government's motion to dismiss. Judge Green called the parties to court for an oral argument on December 1, 2004. Early in the argument, she told Brian Boyle, the government's lawyer, that she wanted to run some hypotheticals to test the government's position about who could be deemed an "enemy combatant" subject to detention at Guantanamo. He smiled, probably to hide feeling a little queasy about hypotheticals, which are almost never a lawyer's friend when posed by a judge.

"A little old lady in Switzerland who writes checks to what she thinks is a charity that helps orphans in Afghanistan but really is a front to finance al-Qaeda activities. Would she be considered an enemy combatant?" asked the diminutive, then-seventy-six-year-old Judge Green.

Understandably, Boyle tap-danced, talking about how it would depend.

"But would she be taken into custody?" Judge Green persisted.

"I think she could," Boyle said.

"How about a resident of Dublin who teaches English to the son of a person the CIA knows to be a member of al-Qaeda?"

"I think he could," Boyle answered.

Judge Green also asked about the amount of time for which enemy combatants could be held. Boyle's answer, essentially, was that the president would decide. In other words, detention would be indefinite and potentially forever. (In fact, there are still uncharged detainees at Guantanamo in 2025.)

If you boiled it down, the government's position was that it could (1) detain foreigners who had not knowingly done anything against the US, wherever those foreigners were found around the globe; (2) hold them at Guantanamo for as long as it wanted as "combatants"; and (3) subject them to treatment we would scream about if inflicted on US personnel—all without any court having authority to say anything about it. Of course, Guantanamo had been picked to house the detention operation precisely because the government anticipated that it would have this form of limitless power there.

But if this is what the law allowed, what point was there in the law? And this was in the context of a presidential administration whose national security acumen had led it to start a massive and already disastrous war in Iraq based on the falsehood that Saddam Hussein had weapons of mass destruction he might use against the US. *That* administration wanted to have unlimited authority to arrest little old ladies in Switzerland and teachers in Dublin, and hold them forever while smacking them around or worse during interrogations? It didn't make sense from a strategic or practical perspective, even if you didn't care about the law.

Listening to the government's arguments in court that day, I wondered how I might explain to Jaber (and other clients) just how extreme the government's position was. Also, if the government somehow won, we likely would never be allowed back to Guantanamo or even to write to our clients. After all, if you have no rights, you certainly are not entitled to a lawyer. Considering Jaber's suicide attempts, I thought that dashing whatever hope might have been raised by my visit by never returning would be devastating, especially if I couldn't explain to him what had happened. We would just have to wait for the court's decision to see if any of those scenarios came to pass.

Putting those legal issues aside, I continued to wrestle with questions about whether Jaber's descriptions of abuses during our first meetings had been accurate and whether he had done anything to warrant his being locked up. Considering that the detention operation had been housed at Guantanamo to protect it from all scrutiny, it was remarkable that a series of documents began to trickle into public view relating to that first question.

In late December 2004, a court ordered the government to produce materials relating to Guantanamo in a case brought under the Freedom of Information Act. Some were emails and memoranda written by FBI agents who had observed and participated in interrogations at Guantanamo.

I sat at my desk one day paging through the documents. I found an email by an FBI agent who had seen a detainee in an interrogation room with an Israeli flag draped on him. There was no mention of the detainee's name, but the email suggested this was not an uncommon practice, presumably because some genius had decided it would be a great way to break Muslim prisoners. I remembered Jaber telling me about being wrapped in an Israeli flag. I had wondered whether he was just throwing propaganda at me. Now, at the very least, I knew definitively that this technique was used.

There was a memorandum by an FBI agent memorializing an interview he had conducted with an unnamed detainee. The detainee had reported being beaten unconscious by an Immediate Response Force. The description of the incident in the memorandum was basically identical to the description Jaber had given me of his IRF beating. At the end of the memorandum, the agent wrote, "Detainee had what appeared to be a recent wound on the bridge of his nose." I could picture the scar on Jaber's nose that he said came from the IRF.

Jesus Christ, I thought, *he was telling the truth*.

I would become even more convinced. Around the same time, *60 Minutes* did a story about Sean Baker, a US solider who had worked at Guantanamo. For purposes of an IRF training exercise, Baker had played a noncompliant detainee hiding under a bunk, complete with orange jumpsuit. The IRF team, which did not know Baker was a US soldier or that they were participating in a drill, dragged him out and beat him so severely he became disabled. According to Baker, IRF interventions were always filmed, but the tape of this incident had vanished.

Then the Associated Press reported on an analysis the military compiled from reviewing the videos of IRF interventions. According to the report, there were many cases of excessive force and taunting. Any doubts I had about the essential truth of Jaber's description of his IRF incident had vanished. He had been the victim of a sadistic beating, period.

As to the question of what, if anything, our clients had done, our next step came in early January 2005, when we first visited the "secure facility" in the Washington, DC, area (to give a more precise location would be impermissible). It was there that the government was keeping all classified information relating to the detainees that it planned to share with habeas counsel. Only lawyers with security clearances could visit.

We had already been given the unclassified summaries of allegations created through the CSRT process, which had been the basis for my discussion with Jaber about the accusations against him. Now, my colleague Mark Sullivan and I were going to look at the classified evidence—the stuff that was so sensitive it could never see the light of day.

I had been anxious about this. I knew we were representing people as a matter of principle. If the government wants to lock up people potentially forever, there should be some kind of process. Even if there is a fair basis to lock up someone, the person still should not be subjected to treatment we would consider torture if a foreign power inflicted it on Americans. I believed that. But from a purely personal perspective, I didn't want to represent a true terrorist. I didn't want to represent someone actually responsible for 9/11. The night before heading to DC, while riding in a cab past the World Trade Center, I had thought about what I would do if that turned out to be the case.

As we approached the secure facility the next morning, I wondered if we were going to find a recording of a conversation between Jaber and an Al Qaeda operative picked up from a satellite phone or maybe a photo of Jaber with fighters at Tora Bora. I felt my stomach in knots.

The facility itself was in a remarkably nondescript office building amid many other remarkably nondescript buildings. Down the hall from the office that housed the facility there were other offices housing businesses with implausibly vague names on the door that were always closed. It all screamed "covert."

Inside the facility, the window shades were drawn, the paper shredders cut horizontally as well as vertically, and the walls were bare—with one exception. There was a Burger King poster announcing various rights of customers, including the "the right to mix Coke and Sprite," "the right to have that big meal sleepy feeling when you're finished," and "the right to dip your fries in ketchup, mayonnaise, BBQ sauce, or mustard." A handwritten asterisk appeared next to the list with a corresponding note at the bottom of the poster, reading, "Not all rights may be available to Guantanamo detainees." I later learned that Marc Falkoff, another habeas lawyer, had done the honors. Baher Azmy and I later took to calling Marc the "wizard" for his never-failing ability to recall the smallest of litigation details on demand when needed—with documents to back it up. I chuckled to myself every time I saw his annotation on the poster.

It took a while for us to get oriented, but eventually we retrieved our clients' files from the facility staff and found a secluded office to review things. We had to make sure that no other lawyers saw our material since classified information is shared on a need-to-know basis. We had yet to challenge the government's position that no counsel could ever need to know anything about another lawyer's clients.

Mark and I each opened a file and spread the contents out on a table. I had picked Jaber first. Almost not wanting to look, I held the relatively few pages in my hand and began reading.

I have to stop being so melodramatic, I thought.

While I can't say what was in the files, I can say what was *not* there. There were no fingerprints, no DNA samples, no voice print analyses, no photographs, no intercepts of communications—just nothing that could legitimately substantiate the allegations in the CSRT beyond what Jaber had admitted to. I breathed a sigh of relief.

I opened the files of two other clients, both of which were even more bare. Mark reported the same from the files he reviewed. If we ever got in front of a judge in a legitimate hearing, this stuff would not be hard to deal with.

As my anxiety faded about whether our clients were legitimate jihadists, it was replaced by an increasingly familiar surge of anger. Even if you don't believe in due process or the rule of law, it was outrageous that people were being detained based on this kind of information, let alone indefinitely. Again, you had to wonder from a purely strategic perspective why the government would want to do that.

Those questions were only underscored by comments that military officials kept making. Army Brigadier General Martin Lucenti, who worked at Guantanamo, told the *Financial Times* that "of the 550 [detainees] that we have, I would say most of them, the majority of them, will either be released or transferred to their own countries. Most of these guys weren't fighting. They were running." General Jay Hood, who ran the entire detention operation, told the *Wall Street Journal*, "Sometimes, we just didn't get the right folks."

While at the secure facility, we also looked at our notes from the Guantanamo trip. These were the notes we had given to Gunny for transport to the facility because they contained presumptively classified information. I read through the twenty-five pages of notes that I took with Jaber, seeing again the details of the IRF beating and the Israeli flag incident, among others.

I looked for my notes from the second client I had seen during the trip. They weren't in the stack of things I had been given by the facility's custodian, so I went to ask him where they were. He double-checked in a room full of file cabinets with heavy locks and reported there wasn't anything else related to our case. Back at the office, I contacted the government's lawyers and asked them to check with Guantanamo. About a month later, I received a letter from the lawyers. My notes, which were not only attorney-client-privileged but also so sensitive as a matter of national security that they warranted classified status, had been "lost in the mail." Initially I was a bit stunned to learn that the government, which took care to keep the notes in a Kevlar bag overnight when we were at Guantanamo, just threw them in the mail for DC. I also was surprised that, beyond saying the notes were "lost in the mail," the government had no plans to address the situation. So maybe the government didn't really think our clients were sharing state secrets with us, since that information presumably was bouncing around the US postal system. Needless to say, the notes were never found.

A few weeks later, I returned to Washington for a deposition in a dull commercial case. Taking advantage of the trip, I went to the facility again—this time with Karim, our interpreter —because we'd been told that letters from our clients had arrived. The government held client letters in the facility because, just as anything our clients told us in person was classified, anything they wrote in letters was also classified.

Jaber, as I might have predicted, was a good correspondent. He had written two letters to me just a few days after our meetings. The first letter said simply that he was writing as I had asked to test the mail system.

The second was much longer. Jaber wrote that other detainees had yelled at him for signing a document I had brought to Guantanamo, which authorized us to represent him.

I don't doubt who you are, but my current situation has made me suspicious even of myself. I have not seen your identification or anything to prove you are a lawyer. I am sick from everything that is going on in my mind. Please send me a copy of your personal identification. Please send me a letter in your handwriting that says the document I signed is simply to retain you. Your letter should have your signature. I thank you and appreciate it. You will save me from thinking and relieve me from the sickness and pain. Please don't get annoyed by this letter and don't consider it a lack of trust. Please forgive my impoliteness in expression. Nobody can act as he is in Cuba. I feel sick and the situation will get worse if you don't reassure me.

Digging through our file, I found another letter, dated after the first two:

This is my seventh letter to you and I have not received an answer. I do not know why I have not received an answer. I am compelled to write because the interrogators have asked me to take a polygraph and voice print. Please send me an urgent reply with your opinion on this issue because I am afraid if I refuse, they will mistreat me more than what I am going through now. If you don't want to answer, that is understandable and I will not disturb you again by my correspondence.

On the one hand, it was something of a relief that Jaber had wondered whether he could trust me. It meant that I wasn't the only one at our meetings who had battled doubts. But the thought of Jaber, sitting alone in his cell, terrified that I had duped him felt awful. The last thing I wanted to do was pile anxiety on someone who had been suicidal. That I had been writing letters to Jaber and our other clients that obviously weren't getting delivered didn't make me feel any better.

I wanted to call Jaber, but telephone calls to detainees were not permitted. I wanted to head back to Cuba, but that required weeks of advance notice. All I could do was send another letter.

On January 31, 2005, Judge Green issued her decision. She denied the government's motion to dismiss our cases, finding that our clients were entitled to fair hearings and that the CSRTs were not that. It was great news. The terrible news was that Judge Green stayed her ruling to allow the government to appeal. Basically Judge Green was saying that these were weighty issues and a higher court should rule on them before her decision would be implemented. That meant a long round of brief writing and oral arguments before the DC appeals court, without even a chance that anyone would get a hearing anytime soon. It didn't bode well for someone like Jaber.

Beyond the delay, Judge Green's decision suggested something else. Obviously she had been sympathetic to the idea of due process for our clients and believed the Supreme Court's ruling in *Rasul* required her to find that our clients were entitled to such process. But even she was not prepared to let court hearings proceed on individual cases. That highlighted a question that had been plaguing some of us since the litigation began. With the specter of 9/11 still hanging over the country, including questions of how the FBI, CIA, and others had failed to track the hijackers, would any judge order that a Guantanamo detainee be released over the government's objection, even in the absence of valid evidence? In a country that still felt the pain of 9/11 acutely, what human being clothed in black robes would be willing to order the release of a person when there was a chance of being wrong? I had not been particularly optimistic about that prospect, and Judge Green's decision to stay her decision made the prospect even dimmer.

Given that it would take many months to get a ruling from the appeals court in DC, and our continuing questions about whether any judge would ever release a detainee, litigating our cases was not going to be enough. We needed a plan B. We needed something beyond the courts.

As I became more familiar with Guantanamo's workings, I saw that detainees from Western countries were being sent home one after the other. Even those who were accused of being very bad guys got to go home if they came from places such as England or

France (which also might have shown that the government didn't really believe its own allegations). In mid-January 2005, the US sent home an Australian who had been accused of training the 9/11 hijackers in martial arts. A month later, a detainee from the UK who allegedly had cased "Jewish" sites in New York as potential targets was transferred out. Meanwhile, we had clients accused of things such as meeting an unidentified man who later was on some unspecified front line. Why was it that the Aussies and Brits could go home and our clients couldn't? From what I could tell, the key was being from a country allied with the US that would seek agreements with the US government for the return of its citizens.

Our plan B had to involve making this a political and diplomatic issue. Obviously Bahrain is not a Western country, and it's hardly a place the average American thinks of much. But as I learned, it was a critical US ally. Bahrain hosts the US Navy's Fifth Fleet, which patrols 2.5 million square miles of water, including the Persian Gulf and Arabian Sea, as well as crucial choke points like the Strait of Hormuz and the Suez Canal. If you're interested in the free flow of oil in global markets, this is key geography.

Considering that Bahrain was a major security partner of the US, why wouldn't it be able to pull strings as other close US allies had to bring its citizens home? Why hadn't Bahrain done that instead of sending security delegations to interrogate our clients at Guantanamo?

In February 2005, I met with Nabeel Rajab, a prominent Bahraini human rights activist who was visiting Washington, DC. Nabeel was instrumental in getting authorizations from our clients' families to commence the habeas cases. I thought he might have insight on my questions about Bahrain.

Nabeel was a warm and fascinating guy. He came from a long-established family in Bahrain and had been a small business owner early in life, doing well in a range of endeavors. Despite that success and coming from relative privilege, he became seized by a passion for human rights, given the dynamics in Bahrain.

As I had been learning, the ruling family and power structures in monarchical Bahrain are populated by Sunni Muslims, while a majority of the population is Shia. To maintain power over the years, the government has engaged in oppressive practices against Shia (and others) who speak out for things such as democracy or humane treatment of prisoners. The government's argument often has been that it needs to engage in tough tactics because Shia citizens want the country to be taken over by Iran, another Shia-majority country. Little proof of that has ever been supplied.

Nabeel was decidedly secular in orientation, but his family had Shia roots. He had gotten grief from the Shia community for helping our clients because they were suspected Sunni terrorists, and Shia often have been the victims of Sunni-dominated groups such as Al Qaeda. But for Nabeel, it was a matter of basic human rights, and he was willing to take that heat. In fact, he was interested in talking now about what else he could do to help our clients.

We discussed that, while Guantanamo was viewed as a scourge internationally, including in Bahrain, there had not been much pressure on the Bahraini government to bring its citizens home. To an extent this was because a big chunk of the population (the Shia) was wary of anyone said to be affiliated (fairly or not) with Al Qaeda and therefore unlikely to take up the banner for our clients. Also, public pressure is harder to generate in a real monarchy than, say, in England. But Nabeel reported that space for political expression had been expanding and repressive practices receding a bit in Bahrain. Moreover, our clients being Sunni was an advantage because they shared that demographic with those wielding power in the Bahraini government.

Admittedly it was a lot to take in, especially for someone with no background in the Middle East. At moments, I wanted to make a chart to keep track of who was in which sect, which group was running Bahrain, which group objected to Nabeel's advocacy for our clients, and so on.

Ultimately we came up with a basic plan. We would try to raise the profile of our clients in Bahrain. That probably could be done through various media outlets in the somewhat free Bahraini press.

We also would try to identify allies in parliament or other high places that might take up our cause. Hopefully all of that would lead to public and political pressure that would encourage the Bahraini government to do the right thing, meaning reach out to the US and get its people back.

With that, plan B went into effect. I began to email Nabeel information about our clients, tailored for a local Bahraini audience. The day after each email, stories would appear in English and Arabic dailies in Bahrain. Then journalists from Bahrain and the Gulf started reaching out to me as they wrote Guantanamo stories, making me feel more like a press agent than a lawyer. The obvious advantage of this strategy was that it did not depend on the courts. Or to put it more precisely, if something bad happened in court, that would be fodder for a story about how the US legal system would never release our clients who thus had to rely entirely on the Bahraini government to save them. I liked to think it was a page out of the Joe Margulies playbook. I also thought Jaber would appreciate the approach.

Chapter 5

WHAT CAN I DO TO KEEP MYSELF FROM GOING CRAZY?

We made our second trip to Guantanamo in March 2005. Stewart Aaron, who had come on the initial trip, was now with another firm. Mark and I divided up Stewart's two clients, so going forward we would each handle three people.

The additional client I took on didn't say anything during our meeting except "I don't want a lawyer," as Stewart had warned he might. I spent the four hours we had in a series of monologues about why his family wanted him to have lawyers, the status of the litigation, and our plan B. When I ran out of things to say about those subjects, I moved to sports, which his father had told me was a big interest. I talked about the English Premier League, how there was an American sport called "football" that didn't involve kicking a ball much, my brother's triathlons, and playing baseball myself. I also talked about what his dad had been doing at the gym, information I purposefully gathered in advance.

"Your dad did eight reps on the bench press at eighty kilos after a long work shift and without eating much. That's impressive, especially at his age."

I had done rough math to convert kilos into pounds, so I knew about how much it was. Karim wasn't a gym rat, though, so I had to mime what I meant by "bench press."

As Karim translated each thing I said, I tried to come up with the next line, hoping that at some point I might say something to spark conversation. It never happened. But at least we didn't get kicked out. And, obviously, the client had agreed to come to the meeting. It was when a detainee told the military he didn't want counsel or refused to go to an attorney-client meeting that a lawyer was fully cut off. For now, I was happy enough to do my monologues, even if it was a bit exhausting.

My time with Jaber was challenging as well, not because he didn't talk but because of what he had to say. He apologized for having doubted me in his letters and tried to explain his anxiety. Interrogators had told him that the habeas lawyers were liars and the authorization form he had signed proved the charges against him. Other detainees were saying that interrogators had told them the lawyers really worked for the CIA. Nobody knew what to believe. "Don't talk to lawyers," a detainee had warned Jaber.

"Jaber, don't apologize," I said. "I can't imagine how suspicious of everyone I would be if I was locked up here. If you ever need anything from me to prove who I am, just ask. And please, don't apologize for it."

Jaber nodded and said that he had finally received my letters. It looked like we were back on track.

After putting baklava and some other food on the table, I brought Jaber up to speed on our litigation efforts. He was excited that Judge Green had decided he and the other detainees were entitled to fair hearings. That excitement faded quickly, though, when I explained that her decision had been appealed and the appeals process could take months or longer. But there were other things he wanted to tell me about.

Jaber said that he had been in solitary confinement for sixteen months, first in Camp Delta and then in Camp 5. In Camp 5, he spent twenty-two to twenty-four hours a day alone in a solid-wall cell with a narrow opaque window. Jaber tried to communicate with other detainees by yelling through the food tray slot in his cell door, which sometimes worked, except if the slot was closed or guards ran loud fans in the hallways, which often happened.

Jaber said he went to exercise in a small, caged pen once or twice a week. Sometimes detainees who spoke Arabic were there in other pens. But other times, there were Afghan detainees Jaber couldn't communicate with, or the space was deserted. Besides those short sessions and the occasional interrogation or shower, Jaber spent every waking moment in his cell. There, the only reading material he had, other than censored family correspondence and my letters, was the Qu'ran. Jaber had memorized it entirely a year earlier. He asked guards for an English dictionary just to have something else, but he was told it was prohibited because detainees were not supposed to learn English.

Jaber's body wasn't faring well either. He had trouble focusing his eyes because he almost never had a chance to look at anything more than ten feet away. A doctor told Jaber he was nearsighted, but said, "We don't manufacture glasses here." (Jaber later got glasses, but the prescription never seemed right.) Jaber also suffered from dizziness, stomach pain, heart palpitations, and numbness in his arm.

At one point, Jaber looked me in the eye and asked, "What can I do to keep myself from going crazy?"

There was no good answer. I couldn't imagine any judge would direct the military to change Jaber's conditions of confinement, and it's not as if I had some other way to influence his daily routine. There were mental health staff at Guantanamo, but interrogators had told Jaber that the "psych doctors" were involved in interrogations, so there was no way Jaber could trust them. What could I possibly tell him?

"Jaber, if you're alone and you feel like you really need to talk, tell a guard you have to write to your lawyer. When he gives you paper, put down everything you would say to me if I was there. Just pretend you're talking to me. I promise I'll read what you write and write back. I also want you to remember that in any moment when you feel alone, there are people thinking about you and praying for you. In Bahrain, in Saudi, in the United States. So, really, you're never alone."

Would those words have had any effect on me if I were in his shoes? I didn't think so. Did I sound like a bad *Afterschool Special*? Probably, but I couldn't think of anything better.

During another meeting on that trip, Jaber pulled away from the table as he had during our first visit to Guantanamo and put his head in his hands. His voice became very quiet. In excruciating detail, he described being interrogated naked in Afghanistan. He said that soldiers had somehow injected gasoline into his rectum. He hadn't discussed this during my first trip to the base because he wasn't sure if he could trust me.

Jaber spoke with devastating conviction, and his shame was palpable. Then he stopped. In a quiet voice, I tried to say he shouldn't feel ashamed about anything he had told us. I said people who perpetrate the abuse, not their victims, should feel ashamed. I think he nodded, but it was difficult to tell because his head remained in his hands. I still heard a skeptical voice in the back of my mind, asking whether military discipline could have broken down that badly in Afghanistan. I thought about the FBI documents I had seen, corroborating the IRF beating and the Israeli flag incident. Maybe it was time to give Jaber the benefit of the doubt.

Speaking of my questions about credibility, Jaber also brought up recent interrogations that related to the CSRT accusations against him that we had discussed before. He said an interrogator had shown him a picture of one of the men he had supposedly recruited near Buffalo, New York. The interrogator said the man was named Sahim and had told the government that Jaber enticed him to go to a training camp in Afghanistan. The name Sahim immediately rang a bell, and I checked my notes.

In fact, I had planned to tell Jaber about an interview that Sahim Alwan, the "Sahim" in question, had given to the press. Alwan said in the interview that he had never met Jaber. He said also that someone named Kamal Derwish, whom he had known for years, was the one who convinced him to go to Afghanistan. It had been publicly reported that the CIA killed Derwish with a missile in Yemen in 2002, so Derwish might have been a real player. This whole interview had caused me to question even more the CSRT accusations. I wondered why an interrogator would bring up Sahim specifically, considering Sahim had publicly disavowed knowing Jaber.

Jaber told me also that an interrogator had recently said that some unspecified people had seen Jaber at Tora Bora (where the CSRT had accused Jaber of "bring present").

Jaber asked the interrogator, "Were you one of them?"

"No, I know you weren't there," the interrogator had replied, backing down.

It would have been a strange exchange if Jaber was reporting it accurately. But it underscored for me that the government had little, if anything, to back up the Tora Bora theory.

Of course, Jaber didn't want to dwell on himself exclusively. He asked if I was still eating molokhia with my girlfriend's family. I told him the relationship had ended a month earlier. He wanted to know why, and I talked vaguely about "issues" and where people are in their lives. In truth, I hadn't felt much like talking about the breakup with friends at home and, in a way, Guantanamo had been a respite from that personal saga. Jaber seemed to understand and didn't press me.

While working on Guantanamo was a useful distraction generally, the novelty of being on the base had worn thin by that second trip. It was replaced by a sense of anger that would build during the day. I was pissed that we couldn't get our clients a hearing and that we couldn't do anything to improve their lives, no matter how small. Even running for an hour in the Cuban heat every night didn't do much for my emotional equilibrium. I had no idea then that I would make ten more trips to the base.

Chapter 6

MANAMA IN THE SPRING

After having met with the Bahraini human rights activist Nabeel Rajab in Washington, DC, I had written to the Bahraini embassy, asking to talk about our clients. A polite and perfunctory meeting followed. A Bahraini official expressed grave concern, said that Bahrain had been monitoring the situation, and promised in only the vaguest terms to follow up on the situation. As far as I knew, nothing had been done since.

Given that no diplomatic action seemed to be happening and the appeal from Judge Green's order was crawling along, we decided to ratchet up plan B. In June 2005, after coordinating with Nabeel, Mark Sullivan and I went to Manama, Bahrain. We hoped to raise our clients' profile with the public and the government as well as spend time with our clients' families, whom we had only spoken to over the telephone.

For the better part of a week, we were on the tiny island of Bahrain. The country gained independence from Britain only in 1971 and still is loaded with Western expatriates. In deference to them, Bahrain has a liquor store, although a sign on the door warns that no alcohol will be sold to Muslims. I wondered if employees could always be sure who was and who was not a believer. Bahrain prides itself on being a modern financial center, and there are no old markets or mosques. In fact, other than some ancient burial grounds, there is very little that predates the 1960s.

Nabeel seemed to know just about every Bahraini of note, and he told us we had a full schedule. He meant it. On our first morning, we met with various activists. We figured this group might be able to keep our clients in the public eye after we left. Nabeel said that a few years earlier it would have been difficult to have these meetings, but a more permissive environment had come to exist in Bahrain.

Next, we traveled to the National Assembly, Bahrain's elected parliament. The Assembly did not wield any direct power in the Bahraini monarchical system, but its members did have a platform and used it to speak out. We met with members of parliament (MPs), including Abdullah Marhoon and Sheikh Adel Maawda. That Maawda was referred to as "Sheikh" indicated the level of respect given him. We understood he was an Islamist to some extent and took positions on issues such as alcohol sales that were driven by his religious beliefs. Sheikh Adel was welcoming and thanked us for representing the Bahrainis. He said he had previously asked the Foreign Ministry for information about its efforts to bring our clients home, and the foreign minister would be presenting that information to parliament the following day. Sheikh Adel asked if we would be his guests for that presentation.

Great timing, I thought.

We gave the group updates on our clients' conditions and the essentially stalled nature of the US litigation.

"If our clients are going to come home anytime soon, it will have to be through Bahrain's efforts," I emphasized.

After Nabeel took us to a surprisingly good Chinese restaurant for lunch (or was Bahrain known for Chinese food?), we went to a press conference that the Bahrain Bar Association had convened. It was then we started to see how significant an issue Guantanamo could be in this part of the world. Along with many lawyers and activists, the room was filled with journalists from Al Jazeera,

Agence France Presse, and more Bahraini newspapers and TV stations than I would have thought existed in a place with maybe 1.5 million inhabitants. Nabeel pointed out people as he, Mark, and I got settled at a table that had been set up on a podium.

I looked behind us and saw a banner that read Bahrain Bar Association, along with writing in Arabic.

"Nabeel, I don't want to be paranoid, but what does the Arabic mean?" I asked.

The last thing we needed was to unwittingly sit under a sign saying something like "Death to America."

In a deadpan tone, Nabeel said, "Bahrain Bar Association."

I felt a little silly.

Nabeel introduced us, then Mark and I dived into things. Each of us described the specific conditions of three of the clients. We described the US government's legal position, meaning that the US claimed it was entitled to grab anyone it wanted anywhere in the world, call the person a "combatant," and hold the person forever, subjecting the person to whatever treatment it wanted. We talked about challenging that position in court, emphasizing that our clients were simply asking for a fair hearing. But we pointed out that nobody could predict if or when such hearings would be held.

We talked about how every European who had been at Guantanamo was now home, including those accused of serious violence. They had gone home because their governments demanded they be returned. We noted that Bahrain is a close ally of the US and asked why European detainees were now with their families, while our clients, most of whom were not even accused of violence, were still at Guantanamo. We asked: Is it because they're from an Arab country rather than a European country? Is it because no serious efforts have been made to bring our clients home? Is this acceptable?

There were many questions from the audience. There also were a few diatribes offered in the guise of questions that touched on all manner of injustice committed in the Middle East by the US. The disaster of the then year-old US war in Iraq featured often. I certainly could not defend the decision to start that war; we steered everything back to our clients. The press conference ended not because the crowd ran out of things to say, but because the room had been booked for something else.

Abdullah was the brother of Adel, one of our clients. Abdullah worked for British Airways, wore a suit, spoke excellent English, and was easy to get along with. He would spend much of the next few days ferrying us around. After the press conference, Abdullah took us to Adel's home. We met Adel's young daughter. I asked if anyone else was home just as Abdullah's cell phone rang. Adel's wife was in another room of the house, but she did not feel comfortable sitting with men who were not relatives. So, she had called Abdullah, and we told her about her husband through Abdullah on his phone.

Abdullah brought us to dinner at a local Bahraini restaurant; I had begun to wonder if there was local cuisine. I had a tasty shrimp biryani, although I was told later there is a debate about whether the dish originated in Pakistan, India, or Iran. It sounded like a good controversy to avoid. Abdullah said he thought things had gone very well that day and that the Guantanamo issue would be front and center in Bahrain.

The next morning, in our hotel lobby, Mark and I looked through a stack of local newspapers to see if Abdullah was right. The papers that were in English had front-page stories about our clients, referring to them as the "Bay Bahrainis." Other papers were in Arabic, which we couldn't read, but there was no mistaking front-page photos from the press conference and our meeting at the National Assembly. I also got alerts about stories from the regional arms of global news services.

Jaber's brother Amir came to the hotel that morning. It was the first time we met in person. When I saw him, I thought of the Ohio guys I had played baseball with in college, most of whom also played football. Amir wore a baseball hat and short-sleeve shirt. He clearly knew his way around a weight room. His bulk made the fact that he was soft-spoken and kind all the more endearing. Amir was married to a woman from Malaysia, had two kids, and worked for an American company in Saudi.

I did my best to be honest about Jaber's condition without being unnecessarily alarming. I had been giving Amir updates about his brother over the phone, but watching as he teared up made it a different experience. I swore to do everything I could for Jaber, feeling like I had become king of empty promises.

Mark and I left for the session at the National Assembly that Sheikh Adel Maawda had invited us to attend. We sat in a balcony above the parliamentary floor. Abdullah, our client's brother, translated. I generally don't use the word *thundered* to describe how anyone speaks, but nothing else would do justice to the remarks Sheikh Adel directed that morning to the foreign minister.

In a booming (and likely well-practiced) voice, Sheikh Adel railed about the terrible conditions our clients were held in, spoke of the US courts moving at a snail's pace, and accused the Bahraini government of not doing anything to bring its people home, all points we had discussed with him the prior day. Pointing to Mark and me in the balcony, he said we were the only ones doing anything for the Bahraini detainees, and he thanked us profusely. Much to our surprise, the entire parliament rose and applauded.

The foreign minister, who had been invited to answer the inquiries Sheikh Adel had lodged with the Foreign Ministry, looked ashen. I almost felt bad for him—until he started talking. He said there were law firms that wanted to represent detainees just to "put themselves in newspapers," which could only be a dig at us. He also assured the assembled parliamentarians that his ministry was "on the case," and that the king and prime minister had raised the issue with US officials.

The rest of the day was taken up with meetings with other political figures and press interviews before Nabeel took us to dinner. We went to the Dilmun Club, a private establishment that had been founded in 1974, just a few years after Bahrain achieved independence. It felt like a relic from the UK's colonial past. The dining area was filled with people whose English accents were impossible to miss and whose flushed faces suggested they were some number of gin and tonics into their evenings.

Nabeel liked the place because it was not a spot that would be under much government surveillance. After all, few expats were complaining about human rights issues or a lack of democracy in Bahrain. That made it a better venue for him just to relax. We talked through the prior two days while eating meals that reminded you what English cuisine was like before the UK was graced with immigrants. We also made plans for the following day, our last in Bahrain, which was going to focus on meetings with significant government officials.

The first stop was the Ministry of Justice, where we talked to Undersecretary Amir Al Khalifa. He expressed sympathy for our clients. We thanked him, knowing full well that security officials (including from the Ministry of Justice, we believed) had treated our people with hostility when questioning them at Guantanamo. Al Khalifa said the Bahraini government was actively trying to bring our clients home, including by asking the US to transfer them to Bahrain along with whatever evidence existed against them. That way, Bahrain could try them in Bahraini courts. Thinking about the "evidence" we had seen against our clients, I asked if the US had provided any such material. As I expected, Al Khalifa said no. On one hand, the idea of transferring clients from Guantanamo detention to a country without much of a reputation for due process to be tried was unappealing. On the other hand, almost anything was better than the Kafkaesque morass at Guantanamo. Also, it was hard to imagine the US ever giving Bahrain evidence that would warrant trials for our clients, who we hoped increasingly would be viewed with compassion by the Bahraini public and government officials.

Our next stop was the Foreign Ministry, which we thought would have to feature prominently in any effort to negotiate with the US about our clients' release. Undersecretary Sheikh Abdulaziz Bin Mubarak Al Khalifa greeted us in a massive and well-appointed room that probably had seen plenty of ceremonial meetings. He thanked us repeatedly for our efforts and seemed genuinely interested in our clients' well-being. He too reported that the government had asked the US to return the Bahrainis. To be clear, we didn't doubt that requests had been made, but it had to be a matter of degree. If the UK or France had made perfunctory requests, that probably would not have gotten people back. The trick, we figured, was for a home country to emphasize how important transfers were.

Trying to invoke a spirit of diplomacy, I first expressed to the undersecretary gratitude on behalf of our clients for everything the government had done, naming each client. I told him that we would have liked nothing more than to report progress in our court cases. However, we had no idea if or when our clients would get fair hearings. I described Jaber's suicide attempts and the desperation of other clients who had been on hunger strikes and who, at times, didn't even think it worth meeting with lawyers. Given the state of our clients and the delays in the court cases, we told the undersecretary our clients' survival was in the Bahraini government's hands. We emphasized that our clients were aware of this and had asked us to convey their request that the Bahrainis do what European countries had done to bring people home. I stressed that I had assured our clients the Bahraini government would take all these steps.

In short, using near obsequious language, we conveyed that the Bahrainis had to take responsibility for this whole mess if they wanted their citizens to survive, let alone come home. I was sure the undersecretary and others in the government were aware that we had been repeating this theme over the prior few days. I hoped they understood that we would keep doing this through the press after we left Bahrain. The undersecretary said our advice would be treated not as "suggestions," but as "recommendations." I wasn't sure what this meant, but it sounded promising. After an elaborate exchange of final pleasantries, we left.

We spent our last evening in Bahrain at an Egyptian hookah bar and restaurant with Nabeel, Abdullah, and a few others. I pretended that smoking tobacco wasn't bad for you if it came through a hookah, and I enjoyed great mezze. It was difficult for us to gauge how effective the trip had been, but Nabeel and Abdullah said everything had been great. If nothing else, we were doing something beyond just waiting for the courts.

Mark flew home, and I went to Yemen, where local human rights groups and some of the Guantanamo habeas lawyers had arranged a conference. While the conference didn't relate directly to our clients, I was in the neighborhood and thought Yemen would be worth a look.

The Old City of Sana'a, Yemen's capital, was stunning. Ancient mud buildings rose as high as one hundred feet into the air, one right next to the other. Their window frames were decorated with white lime, giving the buildings the look of gingerbread houses. Many of the windows at higher floors had stained glass or were shaded by ornate screens. I had never seen anything like these buildings, which sometimes are called the world's first skyscrapers, given their height and proximity.

I also couldn't remember being anywhere that felt so far from Western influence. The great majority of women wore a niqab, a veil that covers everything but the eyes. The men favored a uniform of a *thobe*, a long white robe, adorned with a blazer and a *jambiya*, an ornamental, curved knife worn in front at waist level. It was a dramatic and new look to me. The men also all seemed to have a bulging cheekful of something. I learned it was khat, a plant said to provide a nice high when chewed. And I didn't see signs of Western culture—be it music, food, or stores—with the notable exception of a Baskin-Robbins I came across while walking around a newer part of Sana'a. It was gloriously out of place.

On that first night in Sana'a, I sat in a café on one of the Old City's warren of streets with some young habeas lawyers who had come for the conference. A few of us were trying to nibble on khat when someone remarked how crazy it was for us to be there on the dime of our various firms. Everyone agreed. There is very little in the way of free lunch for junior lawyers at big firms, let alone trips to Yemen. This was probably a first.

The following day, after some preparation for the conference, I saw Tina Foster, another of those junior lawyers. She was wearing an abaya, a loose robe worn by many Muslim women, including in Yemen. I was puzzled since this wasn't her normal garb. She explained that her luggage had been lost, and she couldn't find anything else to buy near the hotel.

We decided to take a stroll around the Old City, which seemed to have endless possibilities for exploring. We came across tons of kids playing in the streets who wanted to walk with us, smiling and trying out their few words of English. We found an art gallery, and I bought an impressionistic painting of Sana'a from the engaging owner. An American prosecutor I worked with in Kosovo had turned me on to the practice of buying a piece of art when traveling, especially when off the beaten path.

But as we walked around, I started to pick up what I thought were some borderline hostile glances from men we passed. *Don't be that person*, I thought to myself. I couldn't shake the feeling, though. At one point, I looked over at Tina. Her family was originally from Iran. Particularly in an abaya, she didn't look like she had just stepped out of a Norman Rockwell painting. I started to wonder if the local men were viewing us—a man who they knew wasn't from around there, with a woman who might have been from somewhere around there—as a couple. That probably wouldn't play well.

"Hey, Tina," I said quietly. "Can you talk loud enough for people to hear you?"

The sound of Tina's unmistakably American English did the trick. We finished our tour at one of the gates to the walled Old City, chatting with some local cops. One laughed as he put the strap of his AK-47 around my shoulder. I felt practically at home.

Flying back from Sana'a after the conference, I pulled out a book I had with me. It was by Erik Saar, a former Army soldier who had worked at Guantanamo as an interpreter. The book was interesting throughout, but it stopped me in my tracks when I turned to page 100.

Saar described rushing to the scene of an emergency in Camp Delta, where he saw a Bahraini detainee named "Halim," bleeding on a stretcher. Saar was called into a nearby shower to interpret Arabic writing that had been scrawled on the wall in blood. It read, "I committed suicide because of the brutality of my oppressors." These were the same words Jaber told me he had written on the shower wall in his blood after a suicide attempt. Halim was a pseudonym—Saar was plainly talking about Jaber.

A page later, Saar described Jaber's IRF beating in Camp X-Ray. He wrote that Jaber's face had been "black and blue." Guantanamo was designed to operate beyond all scrutiny, yet I had more corroboration of things Jaber had described than I did in some of my commercial litigation cases.

We were scheduled to visit Guantanamo starting July 6, 2005, a few weeks after I got back from Yemen. Knowing how isolated Jaber felt, I wanted to see him as regularly as possible.

First though, I had to pay some bills. Mark and I had been representing a hedge fund over the prior year. A second hedge fund had put all its investors' funds into our hedge fund. Why would investors pay two sets of fees basically for one investment? I didn't know, but hedge-fund investing was too rich for my blood. The second hedge fund requested a withdrawal of all its funds at a time when it was contractually precluded from withdrawals. Our client refused.

The second hedge fund brought an arbitration against our client—arbitration being essentially a private court that parties can agree to use. Mark had graciously suggested I take the lead (or "first chair") for the hearings. After a week of opening statements and witness examinations, we were pretty sure we had the other side beat. While it made no difference at all to the universe whether we won the case, my natural competitiveness had me disliking our adversaries and certainly wanting to win. Also, to be honest, it felt like a bit of a respite to work on this matter compared to the charge of Guantanamo. Now we had to draft written statements in place of live closing arguments. After we submitted them, the arbitration panel quickly ruled in our favor.

The day before we were to leave for the July 6 Guantanamo trip, I got a call from the Department of Justice (DOJ). A tropical storm was bearing down on the base, and all operations had been suspended. By the time we could rearrange the trip, three weeks had passed, and it had been nearly four months since I had last seen Jaber.

Although I was anxious about the delay, Mark and I were still feeling a bit of optimism from our visit to Bahrain when we finally arrived at Guantanamo. It didn't last long. Two clients refused to see Mark. One client would have refused to see me, he said, but was too weak to resist when guards had brought him to Camp Echo. Normally he was a tough-looking guy, but he had been on a hunger strike and looked skeletal.

Jaber was not doing much better. He also had been on the hunger strike, which was spreading throughout the camps. His blood pressure was low and his pulse rate high. We talked about the cause of the hunger strike and steps the military had taken attempting to end it. Things were very tense, and Jaber was suffering from nightmares and muscle spasms. He said he wanted to see a psychiatrist, but that they couldn't be trusted at Guantanamo.

I tried to lift Jaber's spirits by telling him about the Bahrain trip and the promises we had heard that action would be taken to get him home. Jaber listened, but he plainly had other things on his mind, including the grim past. He talked about a sexual assault of a detainee by marines that he had witnessed in Afghanistan.

He said also that guards had shackled him to the floor of an interrogation room at Guantanamo during one session. A female interrogator wearing a cross had reached into her pants and smeared her menstrual blood on his body and face. She said, "This is a gift from Christ for you Muslims."

This was one of those things I never would have believed on my first trip to Guantanamo. I mean, American women soldiers were really wiping their menstrual blood on terror suspects? It would have sounded like pure propaganda to me. But several months earlier, a Pentagon report I had never discussed with Jaber described how female interrogators put red dye on detainees, pretending it was menstrual blood. The idea was to make the detainees feel too dirty to pray, which would keep them from accessing a source of emotional and psychological strength: their religion. Whether or not the blood Jaber described was real, again I had corroboration that he was telling me the truth as he knew it, even when it sounded positively outlandish.

Jaber also talked about a Yemeni detainee (whose name I will not use). This detainee told Jaber he had been at Tora Bora and seen Osama bin Laden. He also told Jaber that he had given interrogators the names of over 150 detainees who he falsely claimed were at Tora Bora. "I'll tell them anything to get home," the Yemeni said to Jaber. Other detainees told Jaber that this Yemeni had identified Jaber to interrogators as having been at Tora Bora. One detainee said his interrogator had admitted that the US didn't trust the Yemeni's reporting.

Jaber said all this almost as an afterthought, and for a minute I heard it that way. Then it hit me. The CSRT allegation that Jaber was "present at Tora Bora," though quite vague, was the only allegation that even hinted that Jaber had taken some action against the US. And that was only possible if you made the leap to infer that Jaber had been at Tora Bora during fighting between Al Qaeda and the US and had been part of the Al Qaeda fighting force. But now we knew that allegation was from an entirely unreliable source, someone who openly admitted making things up in the hope of leaving Guantanamo—not that you could blame him. I didn't say any of this in the moment because Jaber was moving on, but it felt huge to me. The case against him just kept crumbling.

As I refocused, Jaber was describing an interrogator who called himself "Jeremiah" and had said to Jaber, "You can't punk me, motherfucker, I'm from Brooklyn."

"Wait, I live in Brooklyn," I said. "What does this guy look like? Maybe I know him."

Jaber laughed.

The "You can't punk me, motherfucker, I'm from Brooklyn" line would become a running joke, with one of us pulling it out at random times.

Jaber had quoted Jeremiah in English, even though Karim was there to translate. It reminded me that there were times when Jaber would say a few words or even a phrase in English. Generally this was to relate something a guard or interrogator had told him. Usually it was off-color.

"Okay, so you know 'motherfucker,'" I said. "What other bad words have you learned at Guantanamo"? I asked with a smile.

Jaber resisted for a minute, looking like an embarrassed school kid, before blurting out, "Honky, wetback, inbred, n****r, son of a bitch, slut, white trash."

Karim grew up speaking Arabic, but had a PhD from an Ivy League university and was utterly fluent in English. Nonetheless, he had to ask, "What's an inbred?"

"You know, it's the same as cracker," I said, smiling at Jaber, who nodded. Karim still looked perplexed.

"Jaber, did you learn all that from the guards?"

"Yes. They use those words all the time, behind each other's backs. The white guards will say, 'That n****r sergeant of the guard,' a black guard will say, 'I hate that white trash corpsman.' The Hispanic guards say, 'I hate white trash and n****rs.'"

Jaber paused for a minute. "But please don't tell my mom that I said those words."

Chapter 7

JUST GIVE ME TEN MINUTES

In October 2005, I was back at Guantanamo. Mark didn't join me because we anticipated that a few clients would refuse to see us, making the interview schedule lighter.

I sat with Jaber first. There was no real progress to report in terms of our litigation, so I started with other news. In fact, I had begun to prepare for Guantanamo trips by cataloging any positive developments I could think of and talking to our clients' families to get any news they had. I told Jaber that one of his sisters and one of his brothers had had babies in recent months. He offered a small smile. I told him that his mom missed him and was praying for him. I said his brother Amir was sending love. I also sent greetings from Karim, our interpreter, who had not made the trip. Abdul, an excellent interpreter I met during barbeques at our Guantanamo lodgings, the Combined Bachelor's Quarters (CBQ), was with me instead. Jaber didn't have much reaction to any of it.

Next, I talked about various media stories that had reported on our case and Jaber specifically—some arranged by me as part of our plan B, and some that came about due to general rising interest in Guantanamo. There were pieces in the Bahraini press, the *Boston*

Globe, Al Jazeera, the *New Yorker*, and others. I told Jaber that one of the articles from Bahrain said negotiations about repatriation were ongoing between the Bahraini government and the US. We had exchanged letters with the Bahraini Foreign Ministry, following up on those reports. Another story from Bahrain reported on a member of the National Assembly who was joining Sheikh Adel to sound the alarm about our clients.

I quickly mentioned that we were still waiting for an appellate court ruling on Judge Green's decision, almost a year later, and had no idea when it would come. Because I felt I had to, I also told him that Congress was looking to pass a bill to throw out of court all the habeas cases. Not wanting to be too depressing, I focused on what the habeas lawyers were doing to fight the bill. In fact, our focus was not on killing the bill, which would have been politically impossible given the unpopularity of our clients. Rather, we were trying to insert language to specify that existing cases could proceed, and only new cases would be barred. I didn't dare tell Jaber what a novice I was to lobbying.

Jaber's normal energy and gallows humor were notably absent. Flatly he told me that Jeremiah was still interrogating him. A different officer had talked to him about the Administrative Review Board (ARB). This was another process created by the government after we filed our cases in an attempt to show that people were getting fair hearings at Guantanamo. The ARBs, evidently, were going to happen each year. They had all the same flaws as the CSRTs.

The ARB officer had described to Jaber the standard set of allegations that we knew so well by this point, with one twist. The officer repeated that Jaber had been seen at Tora Bora, except this time, Jaber had been seen there as a "cook." This was getting preposterous. Since our case started, the military had said Jaber was "present at Tora Bora," evidently on the word of a serial informer whom nobody believed. Now they were adding that he had been a "cook" in a desperate battle set high in the freezing cold mountains of Afghanistan? What would be next? He had been seen shining combat boots there? I suggested Jaber put the whole thing out of his mind.

Jaber also said he had been at the detainee hospital following my prior visit because he had participated in what became a large-scale hunger strike. At the hospital, he had convinced other hunger strikers to voluntarily accept nasal tube feeding. The alternative was to be restrained and painfully force-fed. In a nod to Jaber's efforts, a major had said that if he ended his hunger strike, he would be moved from Camp 5 to Camp 1. That meant going from solitary confinement to a camp where detainees could see and talk to each other. There was nothing Jaber wanted more, so he ate. The military sent him back to Camp 5 anyway. There, Jaber's interrogator yelled that only he, and not the major, could order Jaber's transfer to a different camp.

The isolation in Camp 5 was so unbearable that Jaber had talked to a psychiatrist, despite his complete lack of trust in medical staff at Guantanamo.

"Please, I need help," he had said. "I'm a human being."

The doctor had said she wasn't sure if she could do anything, but she would try. Nothing came of it, and Jaber remained alone in his Camp 5 cell.

I had seen Jaber depressed, but now his affect was almost nonexistent. He could barely smile. At the end of our first day, I said, "I don't mean to sound stupid, considering where we are, but it seems like you're in a really bad mood."

"I am," he replied, looking as tired as I'd ever seen him.

The next day, I met first with the client who normally said nothing except "I don't want a lawyer." Evidently all my gentle haranguing about how much his family wanted him to be represented and how much we wanted to help finally worked. As soon as I sat down, we were in a discussion about his conditions at Guantanamo, our media strategy, his family, and sports medicine; he had been a serious athlete before Guantanamo, and we both had experienced knee injuries. I did everything to keep the conversation going, thinking about how relieved his dad would be to hear that we were connecting. It was one of those little Guantanamo victories.

The next stop was Jaber. We talked a bit more about the hunger strike, but he really seemed to be flagging. He asked to cut things short, knowing I would be back the following day. Also, he said his stomach was bothering him and he needed the bathroom.

To use the bathroom during a meeting in Camp Echo was anything but routine. Guards had to shackle Jaber's hands, release his ankle shackles from a bolt in the floor where they had been attached, and move him to the tiny cell next to our meeting area where the toilet was. The cell was separated from the meeting area by a metal mesh wall. You could see through it, but it was immovable.

"Okay," I said. "Why don't you stay on the other side after you're done, and I'll just come back in to say goodbye."

Jaber agreed. He handed me an envelope, saying we could talk about it the next day. There was nothing unusual about Jaber giving me some writing, but his tone was a little ominous.

"That sounds scary," I joked.

"Yes, *Scary Movie*," he replied, wanly smiling. It was another of his favorite movies.

"Give me ten minutes," he said.

I opened the door to get the guards. A male and a female solider came in, and I described our elaborate bathroom and departure plan.

I went outside to give Jaber privacy. The guards came outside as well after moving Jaber. The male soldier waited with me and Abdul. We chatted about the heat as you did with guards in Guantanamo, and the forecast, which predicted a big storm. It had already started raining.

After a few minutes, I thought I heard the noise of a toilet flushing, but then nothing from Jaber. I started to feel a vague anxiety, although I wasn't sure why. I asked the guard if we should check whether Jaber was done. The guard started to open the door. Immediately we heard a sound that I took to be someone having a real stomach issue.

"That doesn't sound like fun. I guess he isn't finished," the guard said, evidently hearing things as I had. He closed the door.

A minute or two later, not being able to shake my anxious feeling, I walked to the side of the hut where I figured the plumbing would be. I hoped to hear a flush. There was silence.

Starting to think the groan we'd heard wasn't just a stomach issue, I decided to crack the door open, just a few inches.

Looking down, I saw a dark stain on the white floor.

What the hell? I thought, trying to figure out what I was looking at.

It took me an instant to realize it was blood—a pool of blood. I looked up and saw something hanging from the cell side of the metal mesh wall. My mind was scrambling to process information, and I needed a split second to grasp that this hanging thing was Jaber. He didn't look human. His face was covered in blood, his eyes were rolled back in their sockets, and his lips and tongue were swollen. He was bleeding onto the cell floor, and the blood had run onto my side of the wall.

I yelled to the guard, "We need help!"

I took two steps through the blood to the wall. Jaber and I were inches from each other, and I could see him clearly through the mesh. But I couldn't reach him through the mesh, and the door to the cell was locked.

"Jaber!" I screamed.

He didn't respond. He was unconscious and not breathing.

Two guards ran in, including the sergeant of the guard (SOG), whom I had met earlier that day. After first trying a key that didn't work, the SOG unlocked the cell door. He had a knife that he used to hack at the noose around Jaber's neck, which looked like some kind of duct tape wrapped repeatedly.

"Pick him up!" I yelled to the other guard, gesturing to him to lift Jaber's body and ease the tension on Jaber's neck. He wrapped his arms around Jaber's dangling legs and pulled up.

Within seconds the SOG had cut Jaber down and put him on the floor in front of me. Jaber still didn't seem to be breathing. I saw a gapping gash on his right arm, just below the bicep.

"Wrap the arm!" I yelled. I suppose I was trying to say that the wound needed pressure.

"We don't have anything!" the SOG yelled back.

"You gotta get out of here!" he then yelled at me.

I didn't want to leave, but an argument wasn't going to help Jaber. As I walked out, craning my neck to look back at Jaber, I thought I heard him gasp for air.

Another guard escorted Abdul and me to Camp Echo 7, a hut across the compound that was used by the press and occasionally habeas lawyers. When we got inside, Abdul and I looked at each other in shock.

I started pacing the tiny room, suddenly flush with anger. I wasn't angry with Jaber but about the circumstances I knew had driven him to this. Maybe it was easier to experience anger than the other feelings I had.

"Motherfucker," I cursed under my breath a few times. I stopped, not wanting Abdul to think I was cursing at him. We didn't know each other that well.

I remembered the envelope that Jaber had given me. I took it from my bag and began to open it, not that I had any doubt as to what it would be. There were several pages of Arabic writing, stained with dried blood. One of them looked to be a photocopy of a photograph of Jaber and his daughter. I felt chills as I showed the pages to Abdul, not really wanting him to read them. He looked at the letter and just said, "I can't."

I needed to know what was happening across the compound, so I cracked open the door, technically violating Camp Echo rules. I saw nothing except rain in an empty compound. I kept the door ajar. After a few minutes, several people went into the hut with Jaber's cell, one of them carrying what looked like a medical bag. Ten minutes later, Jaber was carried across the compound and out of Camp Echo on a stretcher. It looked like his eyes were closed, and I didn't see him move. The stretcher was bloody on one side. I closed the door.

Two officers came into the room and said they were with Behavioral Health. One was about my age, and the other older. They both looked perfectly nice.

The younger one asked, "Do you have any idea why he would do this?"

Was he serious? This was Guantanamo Bay. There were a thousand reasons to kill yourself here.

"Isolation can do terrible things to people," I said with as much restraint as I could muster, telling myself it wouldn't help Jaber to yell at people who might, in theory, look after him. I reminded them that Jaber had been in solitary for about two years.

The younger officer nodded with more sympathy than I had expected. Maybe I had misjudged his question. Maybe he had just been asking whether anything specific had happened that day to upset Jaber. In any event, they left without another word.

I'm not sure how long it was, but eventually a beefy-looking colonel came in. I was pretty sure it was Colonel Michael Bumgarner, who ran day-to-day operations at the camp. He told me that Jaber had been taken to the hospital and they expected him to recover. I thanked him and asked if I could see Jaber later.

"I don't think that will be a problem," he said.

He seemed genuinely concerned. Almost involuntarily, I felt a surge of gratitude. I needed someone with authority to care about Jaber.

A military lawyer whom I had dealt with before (I'll call him Cruz) offered Abdul and me a ride to the ferry.

"That's not how you want your client to greet you, huh?" he said with a smirk, as we walked out of Camp Echo. I felt like punching him.

"Well, he's been in isolation for two years," I said, probably wanting to defend Jaber and what he had done.

"He's in Camp 5. That's not isolation," Cruz replied.

This was classic Guantanamo-speak. You could be alone in a solid-wall cell in Camp 5, getting out once or twice a week, but if it wasn't explicitly for purposes of punishment, it wasn't "isolation." It didn't matter that you never saw anyone and could barely communicate with anyone.

"He was struggling with the guards," Cruz continued.

"What?" I asked.

"When they were treating him."

I didn't know if Cruz was trying to suggest that Jaber's condition wasn't as bad as it looked or trying to make a comment about hardcore terrorists who would fight even when practically dead. Either way, I knew the person I had seen lying on the floor of that cell, unconscious and bleeding, was not in any position to meaningfully "struggle" with anyone.

I said nothing.

As we drove toward the ferry, Cruz persisted: "I've seen the files on your clients. It would be a mistake to think that they're goat farmers."

I had no idea why he had decided to be such an asshole in that moment. Rather than say what I wanted to about his being a piece of shit and probably a terrible lawyer to boot—what was the point?—I stared out the window.

By the time we got to the ferry, the rain had turned into a downpour and the wind was gusting. The twenty-minute ferry ride was rougher than any I'd been on at Guantanamo. As waves smacked into the sides of the boat, which pitched back and forth, I saw Adbul looking for something solid to hold on to. He said he needed to throw up. I probably would have felt the same way, except I wasn't really feeling anything at all.

When we arrived at the CBQ it was dark. Abdul said he had a bottle of scotch in his room. Scotch has never been my thing, but I accepted because I thought it might quiet my mind, and the idea of sitting alone in my room was terrifying. I felt the burn in my chest as I worked through a couple of glasses. Abdul asked about what had happened. He said that as soon as he heard me yell for help, he moved away from the door to the hut and never looked inside. I tried to describe it, but mostly we sat there, stunned.

When I went to my room later that evening, I immediately reached for the remote control. This was not a time for silence. Above the sound of whatever was on TV, the rain battered the windows. Somehow I got it into my head that if I looked out into the darkness, a disembodied image of Jaber's bloodied face with bulging mouth would be there. I closed all the curtains.

I called Mark and told him what had happened. I said I planned to monitor Jaber's condition as closely as possible and continue visiting other clients. I asked Mark if he thought I was missing anything obvious I should be doing. He agreed with my plan, if you could call it that. We talked about the possibility of the military trying to blame me for any of this. I said I would let him know as soon as possible if it looked like things were heading in that direction. I hoped I'd be able to if that happened.

Around 10:00 p.m., Cruz called. His tone was less confrontational than it had been. He said Jaber had undergone surgery on his arm at the naval hospital, a facility for service members outside the detention camps. He reported that Jaber was stable and sedated. He asked me to write a statement about what had happened. I agreed.

I laid down and turned off the light late that night. It was hard to tell if I dozed at all, but it didn't feel like I was sleeping. By 4:00 a.m., I gave up and turned the light and TV back on. I wrote the statement I had promised Cruz.

At 6:40 a.m., I got on the bus to go back to Camp Echo. I was exhausted and felt a strange mix of numbness and anger; but there were other clients to see. In fact, three of the clients we thought might refuse our visits showed up, and I spent the day running between meetings and also trying to address the situation with Jaber. This was not the right trip to have done solo.

One of the clients I saw was a sharp young guy named Abdullah. He had spent time in college in the States and spoke English well, so it was just the two of us, without an interpreter.

"Why should I have a lawyer?" he asked, right after I sat down. "Look at that clock," he said, pointing to the wall. "I get a clock when I'm in Camp Echo, but I don't have one in my normal cell. Can you get me a clock?"

"You know that I can't."

"So, why should I have a lawyer?"

The question wasn't hostile, but it was firm. I took his point but was too agitated in that moment to concede anything to anyone.

"Look," I said in a tone that was more aggressive than I had expected it to be, "you're right that there's nothing I can do to change your life here except bring you a few snacks. In fact, I promise that you will never see even the slightest change in your life here because you have a lawyer. But there is a lot of work that has to be done in order to get you home, and someone needs to do it. You know that the government of Bahrain doesn't really care about a few detainees here. They would be happy if nobody ever mentioned you again. It's our job to make sure that doesn't happen. It's our job to make sure that everyone in Bahrain knows your name and reads about you or hears about you every day. And if we do that enough, we can get the government in Bahrain to bring you home."

I paused. Abdullah didn't say anything.

"So, you're right," I continued. "You won't see any benefits from our work while you're here. But you will when you step off that airplane in Bahrain."

I didn't know if I'd been convincing or if I was right. It was the best I had.

The next client I saw was on the 102nd day of a hunger strike. It looked to me that he had lost dozens of pounds. For nutrition, guards and medical personnel in the detainee hospital put him in restraints and inserted a feeding tube into his nose twice a day. He reported that this was very painful, but at least the military had started using "10Fr" tubes, which hurt less than the "18Fr" tubes used previously. I made a note to figure out what "Fr" meant; I later learned it was some kind of French measuring system for nasogastric tubes.

Around noon, I spoke to Cruz in Camp Echo. He said Jaber was still sedated. He related that General Jay Hood, who ran the detention operation, had said if Jaber were to wake up and ask for me, the request would be considered. If the commander of the Joint Task Force was making decisions about what would happen when Jaber woke up, plainly the military was taking this very seriously. I was tempted to say I had met General Hood in Kosovo when he commanded NATO forces there (small world), but I wasn't sure how that would play. I just thanked Cruz.

My escort said he had a request to bring me to a military investigator whose office was outside Camp Echo. I wasn't sure if it really was a "request," but I agreed. The investigator—I'll call him Jones—took me into what certainly looked like an interrogation room, complete with a camera. When Jones asked me questions about my address and phone number—the kind of pedigree information police ask for after arresting someone—I wondered whether I had become a suspect.

Trying to test this theory, I asked how long Jones expected our talk to take. He said thirty minutes, so I pointed out that I was scheduled to see several more clients and just did not have the time. I told him I would be happy to talk at the end of the day. I also gave him the statement I had written for Cruz. Jones agreed we could talk later, putting my mind somewhat at ease about whether I was suspected of doing something wrong.

I went back to Camp Echo for another client meeting. On the one hand, I was running on fumes. On the other, being busy and having to focus on people other than Jaber was probably the best thing that day.

In the evening, I called Jones, still a bit worried about whether I was under investigation. Jones said he didn't need anything more from me, which I took as a good sign. I also spoke to Cruz. He said Jaber was still sedated. Again, his tone was friendlier than it had been the day before. He even gave me a phone number I could use to reach him from the States. But given that my flight was scheduled for early the next morning, I wouldn't be seeing Jaber again.

Chapter 8

BEARING WITNESS

I called Cruz from Guantanamo's small airport the next day. He was trying to get an update on Jaber but didn't have new information by the time I had to get on the flight.

For the first and last time, I was the only passenger on the small prop plane that Air Sunshine ran between Guantanamo and Fort Lauderdale. I sat by myself next to the Styrofoam container of soda that the charter company always provided. After your first trip, you realize that drinking anything too early in the three-hour flight could be a problem given the lack of bathrooms.

The storms that had been battering Guantanamo were still in the area. Out the window, the clouds looked like they were two feet away, and rain pounded the wing as we ascended. Turbulence kept the plane bouncing back and forth as we flew around the southeastern tip of Cuba, avoiding Cuban airspace.

I tried to quiet my mind and formulate a plan. Clearly Jaber had wanted to die while I was at Guantanamo so I could be a witness. I could almost hear him saying those words to me. I knew also that Jaber had tried to kill himself because of his desperate isolation. A sense of pressure began to build and expand inside my head as I thought about how I could be Jaber's voice and how I had to get him some help.

I arrived at LaGuardia Airport around 4:00 p.m. It was Monday, so I took a cab to the office in Manhattan. At the very least, I could start talking to people about strategy. Mark had told a couple of colleagues about the suicide attempt. They came by to express concern, but no plans had been made for next moves. I jotted down some ideas and looked through random mail but wasn't making much progress. Having slept little the prior two nights, I realized I was going to be useless, so I went home.

At the time, I was staying with my brother and his girlfriend, now wife. They lived in a converted carriage house in Brooklyn and had offered me their spare bedroom when I moved out of the apartment I had shared with my girlfriend. I got to the house and told them the story, which strangely was starting to come out by rote. Before long, fatigue really set in and I had to go to bed. It was always hard to sleep at Guantanamo, even after routine visits, as I couldn't stop running through what clients had said. But now, for the first time, I had that sensation back in civilization. I tossed and turned for most of the night.

The next day I called Cruz from the office. He told me Jaber was awake, coherent, and "responding to commands." I tried to picture what "commands" would be given to someone who had been a minute or two from death just a couple days earlier. I hoped at least they were delivered gently.

Cruz said also that "people" were asking if Jaber could have gotten whatever he used to cut his arm from me; evidently that item had not been found. I had been waiting for this accusation—or at least the insinuation—since Jones, the investigator, had brought me into the interrogation room. Trying to project calmness and firmness, I told Cruz that I absolutely had not given Jaber anything during our last meeting, let alone anything sharp. I wondered if next the military would accuse me of giving Jaber the material he used to make a noose. That would have been very hard to miss when guards searched my bag before I met with Jaber. If the government wasn't accusing me of that, then it was indisputable that guards had messed up by missing that material in his cell.

That same day, I also started a letter we would send to the government's lawyers at the Department of Justice, asking for changes to Jaber's living conditions. The odds that the military would agree to anything were low, to say the least. As far as I knew, the military had never acceded to any request from a detainee's lawyer about living conditions. They had a stake in keeping Jaber alive, if only to avoid the negative publicity of his death. So we had to try.

My primary goal was to ease Jaber's crushing isolation. I asked the military to move Jaber to a general population area, which he had been in before, so he could see and talk to other detainees. Jaber had probably said a hundred times that sitting alone in his cell day and night made him crazy. Along those same lines, I asked that he be allowed to exercise more than once or twice a week.

Thinking the military or their lawyers at DOJ might view those requests as extreme, I also went for what seemed like inarguably modest relief. I asked that Jaber be allowed to have books other than the Qu'ran in his cell. Jaber had said once that he would love children's books in English and Arabic, which he thought would help him learn English. At that time, we had sent a bunch of titles to Guantanamo, requesting that they be delivered to him: *Cinderella*, *Beauty and the Beast*, *Puss in Boots*, and *Jack and the Beanstalk*. Months later, the books showed up at my office with a sticky note reading "Items not approved for delivery to detainee." Abdullah, the client who had done some college in the US and spoke English well, was a Charles Dickens fan, as he told Mark on an early visit. It was one of our first indications that we should resist assuming anything about our clients. Mark had sent him copies of *Great Expectations* and *Oliver Twist*, which did not make it through either. But now I asked again for permission to send English-Arabic children's books to Jaber as well as Arabic-language novels.

The access procedures put in place by the court for Guantanamo habeas visits said that detainees could watch DVDs from their families that introduced lawyers, provided the military previewed them. You wouldn't want a Bahraini family sending instructions on escaping a Caribbean prison camp, I suppose. The procedures also contemplated that detainees could have phone calls with family members or their lawyers under "special" circumstances. Invoking these provisions, I asked the military to allow Jaber to view a DVD I would have his family prepare, urging him not to hurt himself. I also asked that Jaber be allowed to have phone calls home every couple of weeks. He had not spoken to his family since arriving at Guantanamo, and if these circumstances weren't "special," what would be? Finally, I repeated a request I had made right after getting back to New York that we be given permission to return to Guantanamo on a much shorter timeframe than normal.

The letter asked for a response within a few days, citing the urgency of the situation. DOJ wrote back two days later, much more quickly than usual. Unfortunately the letter began by saying it was unreasonable for us to expect substantive answers so soon. Besides, they said, my letter presumed Jaber wasn't getting proper care at Guantanamo. In fact, DOJ said, Jaber was getting the best care available, and the military didn't need our input. By my count, Jaber had tried to kill himself at least five times before January 2004. After that, someone decided to put him in long-term isolation. Yeah, that was textbook care for a suicidal man. The government also said it was busily considering our request for a quick return visit to Guantanamo but needed more time for that too. Plainly these discussions were going nowhere.

I knew I needed to talk to Amir, Jaber's brother. It was routine that after each Guantanamo visit I talked to our clients' families and let them know how things went. I didn't say much during those conversations because everything clients told us would still be classified at that stage, but at least I could say people were in one piece. Amir knew I had been at Guantanamo and would be wondering why I hadn't reached out.

First, though, I tried to reach Cruz again for an update. Evidently he was now ducking my calls. That was not surprising. I suspected he should not have said word one to me after I left Guantanamo, and I didn't want him to stick his neck out further. The lawyers at DOJ were mum as well, saying I had no right to know what was happening with Jaber.

After a few days of this, I had to call Amir. I dialed his phone, and he greeted me warmly as always. He asked me how I was first, and then asked about Jaber. I made sure he wasn't driving.

"Amir, I want you to know that Jaber is fine, but there was an incident when I was at Guantanamo."

It might have been a stretch to say "fine," but Cruz had told me Jaber was recovering, and I couldn't imagine not offering any comfort to Amir. I hoped it wouldn't come back to haunt me.

Amir didn't say anything.

"Jaber tried to hurt himself," I told him.

I heard fear in Amir's voice. "Jaber tried to hurt himself?"

I explained what had happened in the least graphic terms I could. At first Amir didn't believe it. Jaber was a good Muslim and would never try to kill himself. The military must have done something to Jaber and then tried to cover it up.

"No, I was there," I told him. "I saw it. I know it's hard to understand, but Guantanamo can make people do things that they never would if they were home. I know Jaber would never do that if he was home."

We talked for a while. I kept emphasizing that as far as I knew, Jaber was in stable condition.

"Amir, I think that I need to tell Jaber's story to the public. I think that's what he wants, and I think it's the best thing for his case."

I thought that going to the media with Jaber's near-suicide would be very sensitive for his family. Ultimately we would have to do what we thought best for Jaber, but I wanted Amir to be on board. I explained that Jaber had given me permission to talk about him with the press before. I also said I believed Jaber had done this with me at the base so I could be his witness. To my surprise, Amir agreed immediately that we needed to tell the story. I said I would make sure he had time to talk to his family about what happened before anything hit the media.

I reached out to Mahdis Keshavarz, a press and communications person who had worked on Guantanamo issues. After some discussion, she recommended we go directly to the *Washington Post*. It was in DC, after all, where any and all decisions of substance involving the detention operation were made.

Mahdis connected me to Josh White, a young reporter from the *Post* who she knew was interested. I gave him all the unclassified details. Specifically I could tell him about what I had seen during the suicide attempt and what Jaber had told me about his conditions on prior visits, since that information had been declassified by the government. I couldn't talk about anything Jaber had told me on the last visit since that information was still presumptively classified.

Josh spoke to his editors and thought he probably could get a front page. He asked for a photograph of Jaber. In one sense, it felt macabre to line up press coverage for such a ghastly and, in a way, private episode. But I was sure Jaber wanted the world to know what had happened. I also thought the story could encourage the military to make Jaber's life more bearable. Beyond that, the military had been stonewalling our requests for information about Jaber's physical condition and for a follow-up visit. A big story hopefully would shake something loose. It also could make the powers that be in Bahrain sit up and take notice.

A much more time-consuming and complicated exercise was drafting a motion we would submit to the court, asking it to order the relief we had sought from the military in our letter. I enlisted several colleagues to help. We looked through case after case, trying to find court decisions in analogous circumstances, not an easy task considering that we were dealing with an "enemy combatant" in Guantanamo. We lined up an expert opinion on the effects of solitary confinement from a psychiatrist, formerly of Harvard Medical School. I wrote a declaration, detailing Jaber's conditions as he had reported them to me, and the suicide attempt. All of this was to support a long legal memorandum that would explain our position to the court. To underscore that this was a matter of grave concern, the last line of the memorandum said, "Mr. Mohammed is in grave need of help, but will not receive any absent an order of this Court."

Of course, I still worked at a commercial law firm, and I was still expected to do billable work. And even though people expressed sympathy as they found out what had happened, nobody offered to take any non-Guantanamo work off my plate. So, at the same time, I found myself drafting a motion to dismiss a securities fraud case against a chief financial officer. Slightly different stakes, it seemed.

The pressure I had started to feel on the flight out of Guantanamo had been working its way to a fever pitch. Some part of my mind was always thinking about Jaber and what we could do for him. It was like that from the moment I woke up. I started keeping a notepad on the sink when I took a shower because inevitably some thought about the press angle or our court motion would come to me. The notepad sat on my night table for the same reason when I tried to sleep. Whether I scribbled down anything of value when half asleep or soaking wet is an open question, but it was better to get things out of my head and onto paper.

Months earlier, my brother and I had bought tickets to the Galapagos Islands. We were to leave New York on October 31. It would be the first time off I had taken in over a year, but my initial impulse was to cancel. I realized, however, we could have our court papers and the newspaper article lined up in advance. Nothing would happen directly after we filed the papers with the court and the story ran, so if I got away for a few days, it wouldn't hurt Jaber's cause. I decided to go.

Our flight for Quito, Ecuador, left at 6:00 a.m. I took a nearly complete draft of the court papers with me to the airport. Sitting on the plane at about 5:30 a.m., I left a ten-minute message on the voicemail of a colleague who was helping with the drafts. I described by page and line number various final changes we should make—changes I wouldn't even have thought about making to a normal brief. I felt compelled to apologize in my message for being so tightly wound—or a "hopeless geek," as I put it. On a stopover in Costa Rica, I got an understanding voicemail back, saying the changes had been made and not to worry.

The next day my colleagues filed our motion with the court, and the *Washington Post* ran a front-page article. The article itself led to a lot of additional media interest. I ended up spending the day in my hotel room, doing rounds of interviews. On a purely personal level, it was an amazing catharsis. Finally, I was telling at least some portion of the world about what had happened. And the court had our motion. We were doing everything we could. The pressure that had been building over the prior two weeks in my head broke a little.

I got more relief that evening. A DOJ lawyer emailed to say the military had approved our request to visit Jaber on short notice. This was the request the government had been sitting on for two weeks. I'm sure they would say the positive response had nothing to do with the *Post* story, but pure coincidence struck me as unlikely.

We flew from Quito to the Galapagos, with a stopover in Guayaquil, and spent several days island-hopping on a catamaran. Thankfully—or not, depending on one's perspective—the Galapagos had just hit the internet age, and several islands had places to log on with painfully slow connections.

I was checking in at an internet café when I saw a message from Mark. Three of our clients—Abdullah, Adel, and Salman—had gone home, just like that. I sat there, grinning to myself and dumbfounded. I read the message over and over to make sure I had it right.

I found an Associated Press story about the release. It quoted Sheikh Adel, who had given the rousing talk in the Bahraini parliament during our visit, saying, "The three have arrived and are at their houses." An official from the Bahraini government said, "It was an ordeal for them and their families, which is why we have been working from day one to release them." He spoke also about our three clients who were still at Guantanamo: "We are continuing our efforts with the American government in order to release them and we hope the US will cooperate with us." It was music to my ears, whether the Bahrainis had been pushing for this from day one or had seen the light only more recently. Plan B, it seemed, had worked. Pressure the government of Bahrain and let them get people back. We could see the results. Now it just needed to happen for everyone else.

I wasn't surprised that these three clients had gone first. Two of them had connections to the Bahraini ruling family. The other—a small, friendly man—had been accused only of being a "fighter at Tora Bora." We knew from evaluating Jaber's case that Tora Bora allegations had all kinds of credibility issues. I wondered if the transfer of someone directly accused of doing something hostile at Tora Bora meant that the government itself was backing off from those accusations.

I thought back to a conversation I'd had with Abdullah the day after Jaber's suicide attempt, when he had challenged me to get him a clock. I remembered telling him, "You won't see any benefits from our work while you're here. But you will when you step off that airplane in Bahrain." I smiled thinking about the exchange. I tried to savor a moment of satisfaction. Who knew if or when there would be another.

Quickly, though, my mind drifted back to Jaber. I thought he would hear about the transfer, even if only through the prison grapevine. Would it give him some hope? Or would it make him despair even more for being left behind? I just didn't know.

Chapter 9

THE PURPOSE OF GUANTANAMO IS TO DESTROY PEOPLE, AND I'VE BEEN DESTROYED

Ten days later, Mark, Karim (our interpreter), and I were back in Guantanamo for the visit the military agreed to hours after the *Washington Post* ran its article. We learned we would meet Jaber at the Detainee Acute Care Unit (DACU), which was in Guantanamo's main hospital. There was a medical facility in the detention camps, but the military brought people to the main hospital for more serious treatment. The DACU was a large room with several beds, various pieces of medical equipment, and perpetually drawn window shades.

We weren't in the DACU for medical purposes, though. A small nurses' station occupied one side of the room. Although fully enclosed, it had large windows that allowed us to be watched from close range.

Guards brought Jaber into the room in a wheelchair. He was shackled to it, not that he looked remotely ready to bolt. To the contrary, I had a moment of panic that he was paralyzed. He was sitting motionless in the chair as it was wheeled toward us. He had bruises around his wrists and ankles, and under an eye. The skin on one cheek was hanging down. He wore a neck brace. The last time I had seen him, he had been on the floor of his cell with blood covering his face. He looked better than that, but not by much. When he got near the table that had been set up for us, he gave a faint smile and moved a little in his chair.

We stood around awkwardly as the guards maneuvered the wheelchair up to the table. I gave Jaber a gentle touch to the arm. I didn't think he could take more than that.

"I'm sorry," he said when the guards left. "I'm embarrassed for what I did."

"Jaber, I'm just happy to see you sitting here in front of us. I was scared that might never happen again."

He nodded slightly.

"We can talk about anything you want, but will you tell us how you are physically?" I thought it might help him to focus on something tangible.

"I didn't want you to see me like this. The doctor told me that I have a fracture in my second vertebrae. They operated on me twice. They said I cut 70 percent of my vein. I had fourteen stitches. But I did not hit any nerves."

Jaber's tone was flat. It seemed he couldn't move the left side of his mouth, which made his speech slurred.

"What are your symptoms now?" I asked.

Jaber said he was suffering from severe headaches and spasms that lasted for several minutes. The spasms left him exhausted and made his tongue feel so heavy that he had trouble talking. He said the paralysis to his face came and went. He reported having pain from the back of his head halfway down his spine. On a scale of one to ten, he said it was a seven. His hands and feet felt numb, and he had trouble standing up.

Unfortunately Jaber wasn't doing much to help his recovery. He said he had been on a hunger strike for eight days and was also refusing liquids. A couple of times, nurses had forcibly given him IVs, but at least once he had managed to pull out the tube.

I heard that skeptical voice in the back of my head again. Could someone who had just put his body through the trauma of a suicide attempt even be having a conversation if he hadn't had any nourishment for over a week? Could Jaber even really remember when he had or hadn't eaten?

We urged Jaber to stop the hunger strike—or at the very least to pause it. There might be time for that kind of protest later, but I reminded him that I would be talking to his family when I got back to the States. I needed to be able to tell them that he was recovering. Also, I gently joked, "What kind of meeting would it be if we didn't eat?"

After some back and forth, Jaber agreed to take an IV, saying he was feeling exhausted and might not be able to continue talking otherwise. I had noticed that he kept forgetting Mark's name. With the expertise of someone well versed in hunger strikes, Jaber said he would take the IV that day and then the next day perhaps we could eat together. He would tell the staff that he had agreed to do this just while his lawyers were visiting and that he would revert to the hunger strike when we left. *First things first*, I thought. *Let's just get an IV in his arm.*

I walked to the nurses' station where four or five people were intently peering out the windows at us. I asked if someone could administer fluids. A nurse brought an IV with a stand to our table, accompanied by a few guards. The nurse held Jaber's arm and put the needle into Jaber's skin, probing for a vein. Jaber grimaced. After a few seconds, the nurse pulled the needle out.

"I can't get a vein," he said. "Let's do it again."

He stuck the needle back into Jaber's arm. He was gentle, but it looked painful. Jaber groaned. After a moment, the nurse brought the needle out again.

"His veins are rubbery because he's so dehydrated," he said.

So much for my theory that Jaber was getting more nourishment than he told us.

"Do you want me to try again?" he asked Jaber.

Jaber nodded and pointed to a spot on his arm. "Try there." Obviously Jaber had some experience with this kind of maneuver. After four more tries and several more groans from Jaber, the nurse was ready to give up.

"It's just so rubbery," he said.

I wasn't sure how much more Jaber could take. He had been in visible pain during each attempt. Someone called another nurse, who was able to insert the IV. The first nurse was young and looked upset. I felt bad, and I thanked him several times for trying.

Within moments, Jaber was sharper and more alert. His speech improved. The paralysis to his face even seemed to ease.

He said that a couple of weeks earlier, a female psychiatrist and the head doctor at Guantanamo had threatened to send him from the DACU, where he had been after surgery, to Delta Block, which was styled as a psychiatric ward. Jaber had been there before and knew it housed Guantanamo's truly unbalanced detainees.

"If you take me to Delta, I will not eat, I will break my neck, I will open my wound," he told them. "Take me to the detainee hospital so I can be with my brothers."

Jaber got his wish but was terrified that he would be moved to Delta at any moment. The female psychiatrist said if he did anything to hurt himself, that was where he would go immediately.

I asked whether this psychiatrist was doing anything helpful.

"I don't need mental therapy," he replied. "I need a rehabilitation center to get out of depression and sadness. I need a doctor who is a human being. I need something to occupy my mind."

Jaber said that, still, the only book he had was the Qu'ran. But now he had to read it with one hand, since generally his other hand was shackled to his bed.

We told Jaber about the motion we had filed with the court, describing how we were asking for improvements to his living conditions, including being housed in a general population area and getting additional books. We said it would be an uphill fight, but we had a chance of convincing the judge to give him some help. I didn't want to oversell things, but I wanted Jaber to have maybe a sliver of hope and to know we hadn't just been sitting around.

Jaber thanked us. Before we could talk about our recent plan B efforts, he said that a Guantanamo staff member—he wouldn't identify the person—had read the *Washington Post* article to him. It seemed like he was pleased with the piece. An interrogator had told Jaber that he was famous. I told him there had been articles about what happened in many other news outlets and that we had done radio and TV interviews about it as well. Obviously we didn't want to encourage Jaber to hurt himself for attention, but it seemed important for him to know there was interest in him, and that we had been telling his story.

Jaber was moving quickly between subjects.

"I remember talking with you during our last meeting. I remember giving you the letter. I don't remember anything after that. I don't remember even that you left the room."

"Do you know what happened after I left?"

"Doctors in the detainee hospital told me. One said I was hanging for five minutes. I was very near death, but God did not will it. You have to be thankful to God."

Right, I thought, *God and an anxious lawyer*. But I was relieved to hear Jaber offer thanks at all for being alive.

"What do you remember?" he asked.

I told Jaber that I had found him hanging and bleeding. I said I had called the guards who cut him down. I told him about hearing him gasp for air and watching later as corpsmen took him out on a stretcher. I used the most clinical terms I could in an even tone, figuring Jaber didn't need any more drama or excitement.

"Do you understand why I did this?" he asked.

I nodded.

"I wanted to send a message to the world that Guantanamo is intolerable. I wanted to kill myself in front of you so the military could not conceal my death. I wanted you to witness my death so it would not be anonymous."

His words confirmed what I had known all along. They also stung a bit, truth be told. At moments during the prior three weeks, I had been angry with Jaber even while worrying about him. *What kind of friend subjects you to that?* I asked myself. *What kind of friend would burn that image into your mind?* I knew Jaber acted from desperation, but I had decided I was entitled to my own reaction to the whole thing.

Despite the IV, Jaber was again looking exhausted. We asked if he wanted to stop. He said yes.

That night, Karim suggested I talk to his father-in-law, a doctor, about the best way to bring Jaber off the hunger strike. I was told to start Jaber with a can of Ensure and to be very careful with solid food. Sugar was out. It sounded like good advice.

The next morning we got on the bus to begin our usual hour-long trek to the Windward side. Karim had a big Tupperware container on his lap, which he said had homemade cookies.

"Didn't your father-in-law give us a lecture last night on being easy with solid foods and avoiding sugar?" I asked.

"I will keep them under the table and maybe he can have one later," Karim said.

I was skeptical but also distracted, thinking about the issues I wanted to discuss with Jaber. I forgot about the cookies.

As soon as we got to the table in the DACU, where Jaber already was sitting, Karim put the Tupperware on the table with a thud.

What the fuck are you doing? I thought.

"What are those?" Jaber asked.

Karim explained, and immediately Jaber wanted some. Considering that every Guantanamo client we'd ever seen hungered for junk food, this was entirely predictable.

Mark and I cautioned Jaber that he shouldn't break a hunger strike with cookies, but he wasn't having any of it. He wanted cookies, period. We argued for several minutes. Karim chimed in to say that Jaber was an adult and could eat anything he wanted.

I was ready to bounce Karim off the wall. Mark, always better at remaining calm, pointed out that we were responsible for whatever happened to Jaber during the meeting. If Jaber went into some kind of sugar shock, we would have a tough time convincing the military to let us see him again—ever. And we couldn't let that happen.

"This makes me angry," Jaber said, looking in my direction.

He had never used such an agitated tone with me.

"You know what? I'm mad at you also. I'm mad that you made me see you like that. I understand why you did it, but it makes me mad. So, I think I know what you mean when you say you're angry."

I didn't want to upset Jaber, but I also wanted to make sure I didn't enable his destructive impulses. Maybe if we talked honestly and I didn't treat him with kid gloves, it would help. Unless, of course, it didn't.

"But the thing that makes me feel good," I continued, "is that we can tell each other that we're angry. We can say that and still be friends. We can say that and I will still do everything I can for you as your lawyer."

Jaber nodded. His expression relaxed.

"Anything can push me over the edge," he said quietly and wearily. "I feel like I'm on the brink of collapse. The silliest things make me want to scream. If I ask a guard for something and it arrives late, I get so upset. I put so much effort into organizing my last attempt to die and . . ."

He took a cookie and devoured it, seemingly without chewing. Neither Mark nor I said anything. He took another and wolfed it down. He looked fine. Maybe the conventional wisdom was all wrong.

"I have ended many hunger strikes," he said knowingly.

I let it pass, deciding we had covered hunger strike protocols as much as we could for the moment.

"Jaber, I'm sure that I know the answer to this question, but I just want you to confirm. What would make your life easier while you're still at Guantanamo?"

"Being with my brothers. Being outside."

"That's what I thought. That's what we asked the court for," I reminded him. "But I want you to remember that we aren't just trying to make life a little better at Guantanamo. We're doing everything we can to get you home."

I said that three Bahrainis had just gone home. Jaber knew already, as I figured he would. I told him we were keeping the pressure up in Bahrain, including through the media there, cataloging twenty-six of the stories that had appeared since my prior visit. Some of those articles reported that the king of Bahrain personally had intervened with the US government to bring our first three clients home and that the Bahraini prime minister had ordered government ministers to do everything possible to bring home Jaber and our other two clients still at Guantanamo. It was reported that the crown prince was raising the issue with the US and that Bahraini members of parliament had discussed the case with a delegation from the US Congress. As long as he was at Guantanamo, we told Jaber, everyone in Bahrain would know it. None of this information seemed to resonate much with him.

He looked down and said, "The purpose of Guantanamo is to destroy people, and I've been destroyed. I have no more hope. I can't trust anyone. I cannot be patient anymore. I did the best I could and now I just want to rest."

That night, a military lawyer said we would not be allowed to see Jaber the next day. Another detainee needed to use the DACU. We said that we would be happy to meet Jaber anywhere. The lawyer said a decision had been made that we could only see Jaber at the DACU, and it wasn't going to be available. We asked if they really wanted to tell a suicidal man he wasn't allowed to see the only people he trusted. The lawyer said it wasn't his decision, and we couldn't talk to those in charge. It had to be the fiftieth time I'd heard that at Guantanamo.

A week later, the Department of Justice sent us a letter. On the day after our canceled meeting with Jaber, he took a razor blade to his arm. But they told us that he had survived and was continuing to get the best possible care.

Chapter 10

PIZZA AND CHECKERS

In addition to the letter about Jaber's suicide attempt, the Department of Justice graced us with its response to the court filing we had made regarding Jaber's conditions. The military, through its lawyers at DOJ, said we had things all wrong about the detention operation. In fact, there was no "solitary confinement" anywhere in Guantanamo, and certainly Jaber hadn't been in "solitary confinement" in Camp 5. Rather, he had plentiful opportunities for human interaction.

First, the government wrote, he could talk to guards and "mail delivery personnel" on his cell block. As the government told it, Jaber had "received 51 pieces of mail" since arriving in Guantanamo. In their view, that meant he was able to communicate with his family.

The government claimed further that the feed tray slots in the Camp 5 cells were opened to facilitate communication between detainees during the call to prayer. And even when the slots were closed, "with a raised voice [Jaber] can communicate effectively" with other detainees.

Beyond those robust opportunities Jaber had for meaningful relations with fellow detainees through his tray slot or the solid cell walls when the slot was closed, the government reported that Jaber had "established a cordial relationship with members of his interrogation team." Indeed, during the prior two years, Jaber "had at least 29 interview sessions, which allow [him] to interact with one or more interrogators in various ways, including eating Western food such as hamburgers and pizza, watching movies, playing checkers, or engaging in other informal interactions." It was said that several months earlier, Jaber "had seen the movie *Gladiator* and had expressed a liking for the movie. Because of his expressed wishes, he was shown *Troy*, which has similar motifs."

Finally, the government claimed that Jaber—who they said had attempted suicide eight times—was receiving the best psychological care available. For all those reasons, the government argued that Jaber faced no risk of "irreparable harm," referring to the standard we had to meet to win our motion.

I was enraged by the government's brief. At one point, reading about pizza and checkers, I threw the papers against the wall in my office. First, the government was playing semantical games with the phrase "solitary confinement." Purposefully, we had not used that term in our brief so as to avoid the semantics. Instead, we described the specific facts of Jaber's isolation that led to his despair. Now, no doubt relying on some hypertechnical yet undisclosed definition of "solitary confinement," the government claimed it didn't exist at Guantanamo. That argument probably was wrong even hypertechnically, but it also missed the point about the reality of Jaber's day-to-day life.

Second, the government's characterization of Jaber's supposed human interactions was flat out maddening. Obviously, Jaber spoke to guards from his cell, as the government said. I mean, prisoners see guards. Even in gulags. So what? And the idea that Jaber got to hang out with "mail delivery personnel"? Was the government saying he had nice discussions with those personnel as they threw mail through the food tray slot? How often did he even receive mail? Getting fifty-one letters in four years was a grand total of about thirteen letters a year. Yeah, the mail was really stacking up.

Also preposterous was the idea that a human being is not isolated if he can scream to other detainees through his closed food tray slot, or that without screaming he can make himself heard when the slot is open. And the government didn't address our point that fans in the blocks made it impossible even to yell to others with the slot open. This omission must have meant that there was nothing at all for them to say in opposition.

The most absurdly surrealist point of all was that Jaber had warm, gratifying personal relationships with his interrogators. After the many reports from US government personnel about abuses by Guantanamo interrogators, this argument was nothing short of Orwellian. Were we really supposed to believe that Jaber's inquisitors were just trying to make sure he saw movies with "motifs" that he liked? How truly solicitous. I thought of Jeremiah and his "You can't punk me, motherfucker, I'm from Brooklyn" line that Jaber and I often used on each other. Did he say that during *Troy* or *Gladiator*?

I gave the government's brief to Josh White, the *Washington Post* journalist who had been covering Jaber's case. "If I'd known it was such a slumber party, I would have gotten my own interrogators years ago," he quoted me as saying in a piece the following day. Perhaps it was too glib, but responding in earnest would have given more credit to the government's argument than was due. I also made sure that the Bahraini press had all the details about the government's brief, which turned into a fresh batch of news stories.

Over time, this press work—not the province of most lawyers—had become a rewarding part of the case. Being quoted about an important international issue in the *Washington Post* made me feel less powerless and voiceless and more like I had a megaphone.

But there were downsides to the media attention. First, the public did not see Guantanamo as we did. As opinion polls showed, most people liked having the detention operation. For many Americans, every Guantanamo detainee was a terrorist with American blood on his hands who should be held forever. So I wasn't surprised that threats started coming in. My assistant and I stopped picking up the phone for numbers we didn't recognize, so callers began leaving profanity-laced voicemails, saying I was a terrorist lover and promising to give me the same treatment detainees got at Guantanamo.

Even though social media wasn't much of a thing yet, people also sounded off in chat rooms. Commenting on an article about a suicide attempt by Jaber, someone opined, "Televise it live so we can all enjoy this carpet flyers [*sic*] trip to the land of 72 virgins. At least they didn't have their heads sawed off." LoneRangerMassachusetts replied, "I vote for sending the lawyer's [*sic*] along with the jihad-ist's," while providing my work address.

I know activists who aren't phased by that kind of thing; it's an admirable fortitude I don't have. I found those voicemails and messages disconcerting. For a day or two after each threat, I tended to look around when I was outside and even varied my routes to and from work. Nothing ever happened, and I felt a bit melodramatic after some time had passed. Then the next threat came.

The other downside to media exposure related to the firm. While the partners generally supported our Guantanamo work, including the cultivation of the press, there always was a concern that we might be getting too high profile. After all, we had colleagues who didn't think this was a worthy endeavor. One colleague started referring to us as "Team Taliban," mostly—but not entirely—in good humor. Also, there were paying clients who didn't believe in due process when it came to detainees. At one point I was told a client had moved his business to another firm for that reason. I never got any details, but the danger stayed in the back of my mind.

I found myself talking to the firm's managing partner about these issues one evening outside a Colorado resort where the firm was having an all-office retreat. I knew he was taking some heat for our work. I felt anxious when he brought it up. He was a big guy with a homespun manner, at least to my jaded New York ear. I felt hugely relieved when he said, "Well, Josh, sometimes you just have to say 'Fuck it' and keep doing the right thing."

Indeed. We had a fast-approaching deadline for our reply to the government's papers. I asked a young associate to track down any cases that found interrogation to be an antidote to isolation. She promptly reported this was a novel argument in American jurisprudence. I figured as much but wanted to check so we could make that point in our brief.

I had long planned to speak about the Guantanamo litigation at an Amnesty International conference in London. It was scheduled to take place a few days before our reply had to be submitted. Not only was I going to participate in the conference but Nabeel Rajab, our man in Bahrain, was attending, as were several of the Bahraini parliamentarians who had been working on Guantanamo. It would be important to spend time with them to keep their in-country advocacy going.

I needed another partner in crime for the reply and thought about whom I might try to entice. Lauren Rasmus sat two offices down from me. She was about my vintage, very skilled, and sympathetic to the cause. What I didn't know yet was that her dad, when he was a lieutenant in the navy, had served at Guantanamo during the Cuban Missile Crisis as aide to the admiral who commanded the base.

Having absolutely no authority to demand that Lauren do anything, I poked my head into her office to ask gently if she might have a "little time"—it's my standard, if sometimes disingenuous initial framing of requests for assistance. She had heard all about Jaber's situation and didn't hesitate. It was only then that I started to describe the extensive brief we had to prepare.

We agreed that I would draft an outline of the reply, which she would turn into a presentable brief. This let me go to London and also allowed me to take a three-day trip to Kosovo I had planned to tack onto the end of my UK sojourn. The flight from Gatwick to Kosovo took only a few hours, so the chance to spend Thanksgiving in Pristina with old friends seemed like a great option, as unlikely as that might have sounded to some.

I worked on the outline for the brief until I had to leave for the airport. I slept a bit on the red-eye but kept waking up with fresh language in my head that seemed indispensable to our reply. When

I looked at my scrawl over an airplane breakfast, that turned out not to be the case.

Going through immigration in London on a Friday morning, the agent asked if I was in London for pleasure.

"No, it's actually business. A weekend conference."

"And where do you head to next?"

"Kosovo."

"That must be for business."

"No, that one's pleasure."

He chuckled.

The London conference went well, and Nabeel and I spent a good deal of time making plans to ratchet up the pressure in Bahrain. Lauren faxed me a draft of our response at my hotel. I felt almost weepy with gratitude to see the care she had put into it. She knew how much it meant to me, not to mention Jaber.

Stepping off the plane in Kosovo, I was greeted by the familiar Siberian winds, screeching blackbirds, and smell of burning garbage. I found a cab and rode into Pristina, what you would call Kosovo's capital city, marveling at all the new construction.

My friend Faruk, who had watched out for me during my initial stint there, met me at what had been the first restaurant to reopen in Pristina after the war. We had coffee and caught up before meeting other friends at an endless series of new bars.

Later that night, we climbed ten flights up to his apartment in a Tito-era tower block that had never had a reliable elevator. I lay down on the couch to sleep but couldn't drift off. After an hour I was struck by an extraordinary realization. It wasn't Guantanamo keeping me awake. I wasn't even thinking about Guantanamo. I was just freezing cold because the temperature was in the teens and the power was out. In fact, I hadn't thought much about Guantanamo or Jaber over the prior few hours, the first time that had happened since the suicide attempt. Kosovo was like a private meditation retreat, keeping me in the moment.

It was during my time working in Kosovo that I had first discovered how other people's crises, particularly if occurring in far-flung locales, can be my Zen place. It isn't a great insight to say that people who deal with shock and distress when young can have trouble escaping those sensations later. I certainly found myself confronting general feelings of doom, sometimes around real things that weren't really doom-worthy or even in the absence of any trigger. But in Kosovo, and now in Guantanamo, *other* people were faced with real life-or-death issues, and my job was to try to help *them*. That required an ironclad focus on hazards that existed contemporaneously and had nothing to do with my own issues. The result, I found, was that my attention was fully in the present. I'm pretty sure that's what mindfulness aims for.

Years later I read an article about a psychiatrist who had given a talk at the American Academy of Forensic Sciences. The psychiatrist discussed his experiences working with former Guantanamo personnel. That included a guard who "'cut down a detainee' who tried to hang himself after chewing through an artery in his own arm" with "blood everywhere." The guard ended up having anxiety and panic attacks. Putting aside the misunderstanding about how Jaber cut his arm, obviously this was one of the guards who came in after I yelled for help.

I won't discount the pure horror of what we both saw in Camp Echo that day and how those images stayed in my mind. And, of course, in the immediate aftermath of the suicide attempt, I was feeling a massive amount of pressure. But I never felt close to a panic attack or disabling despair. My focus had to remain on a horrifically compelling external situation. I felt better equipped to deal with Jaber's issues than I did with my own darker personal ruminations. And being in Kosovo again had thankfully summoned the same crisis-inspired equilibrium.

When I got back to New York, the court called to set a date for oral argument on our motion. In layperson's terms, the judge wanted to hear from us and the government in person before deciding what to do. Mark asked if I wanted to make the argument. Although he had more than ten years' experience on me as a lawyer, he graciously said I would do as well as anyone. I wasn't sure about that, but I felt like I had to do it.

The argument was set for early afternoon on Monday, December 12. I spent the weekend looking through the two dozen or so submissions that we and the government had made along with the briefs. I continued to work on an outline of what I hoped to argue in court, knowing an outline always is subject to a judge's interjections at any point. I ran through the arguments to myself under my breath and sometimes out loud. I also tried to convince myself that the argument wasn't particularly important, a psychological trick designed to feel less pressure. *This judge isn't going to give us anything, no matter how good my argument is*, I told myself.

There were flurries when I left for the airport on Monday to get the shuttle to DC. By the time I was at LaGuardia, it was snowing harder. The flight was delayed, but I had booked it for a bit earlier than needed. The flight was delayed again. Then the snow started furiously swirling. Feeling stressed, I called the court to say I couldn't get there. Thankfully the court rescheduled for that Friday with little fuss.

The good news was that we would still get our day in court, and I had more time to prepare. The bad news was I had four more days of trying to convince myself that this was just another appearance in just another case. And you can only run through an argument so many times before it just sounds like a mishmash of words.

We decided that I would fly to DC the day before the argument and spend the night there. We also decided that my colleague, Chris Karagheuzoff, who had been working on the case, would join me in court. It was always good to have another set of ears, and Chris was very sharp.

When I got to the hotel in DC on Thursday, I saw a letter had come in from the government via email. The government reported that Jaber had been transferred to Camp 1, "where he continues to receive appropriate medical and psychological treatment." My rough understanding was that Camp 1 had metal mesh walls between cells rather than solid walls. In theory, this was an improvement and consistent with our request that Jaber have more interaction with other detainees. So, at first blush this was good. But without more detail or talking to Jaber, we couldn't be sure where exactly he was being held within Camp 1 or whether it really made things better. Also, this was a classic Guantanamo move by the government. Refuse all reasonable requests and then, just before a court might get involved, do something to make it seem like the issue is moot.

I showed up early for court on Friday morning. Josh White from the *Washington Post* and a couple other journalists were there, which felt like it upped the stakes even more. My psychological games were getting harder to play. Failing a suicidal client would be bad enough. Having it written about in the press would rub salt in the wound. Chris arrived, and we went into the court room.

I think it's fair to say that those trying to project power tend to build big. It's not as if the Romans, National Socialists, or pharaohs, for example, are best known for quaint or cozy structures. The architects who design federal courts follow this philosophy. While the DC district courts are not the biggest, they are still very large rooms with high ceilings. And the bench where a judge sits is placed on a platform noticeably higher than the floor. None of it is designed to ease attorney anxiety.

Chris and I went in and sat at counsel table. Typically there are two tables for lawyers (or "counsel tables") in a court room. The standard practice is that the lawyers for the party with the burden of proof in a case sit at the table closest to the jury. This tends to preclude arguments about who sits where. But sometimes there are fights about who has the burden of proof and gets to sit closest to the jury.

A moment or two after we sat down, the court room doors opened and eight white guys in dark suits, most of whom looked fairly young, strode in: the government lawyers. They walked toward the well of the court room. A few of the older-looking ones went toward the other counsel table. The rest sat in the first row of the gallery. It wasn't a fair fight numbers wise. I always wondered if these guys were doing the case because they believed in the Guantanamo operation or if they just worked at DOJ and got assigned to it. We shook hands with the lawyers standing by their counsel table.

"All rise."

Judge Reggie B. Walton entered the room. For those who recall that Judge Green denied the government's original motion to dismiss and wonder how Judge Walton became involved, our case was assigned to him at the time we filed it. Judge Walton and all other DC district court judges (with one exception) had initially referred their habeas cases to Judge Green but had taken them back after Judge Green denied the government's motion.

According to an article that profiled Judge Walton, he "grew up on the rough streets of a Pennsylvania steel town" and "occasionally packed a gun and a straight razor and was arrested three times" as a teenager. After attending college on a football scholarship, he went to law school and then became a federal prosecutor. President Ronald Reagan appointed him as a judge to the DC superior court. For a time, he served as President George H. W. Bush's associate director of the Office of National Drug Control Policy and senior White House advisor for crime. George W. Bush appointed him to the federal court. He had a reputation as a "tough" judge, which typically means one who hands out substantial criminal sentences. For a lawyer representing a person who has run afoul of the US government, this is not a welcome profile. I had appeared before Judge Walton a couple of times already, and he did not seem inclined toward our arguments.

Some judges offer at least a perfunctory smile as they enter their court rooms. Judge Walton was not that type.

Chris and I hustled back to our table. Chris has a wicked sense of humor, and there are no sacred cows that get in the way of a good joke for him. Probably sensing my tension, Chris leaned over and whispered dryly, "Hey, don't fuck up. I think we could win some of this."

I felt a little more relaxed, just as he had intended.

Right out of the box, Judge Walton looked at me. "What is the legal predicate for me having the authority to order that the military do the things that I am being requested?"

It was a complicated question, and awkwardly phrased, but one we knew was coming. I said that Judge Green had found detainees to have Fifth Amendment rights in her decision to deny the government's motion to dismiss. I was going to explain that point further and then address other bases on which he could act, when Judge Walton asked how we knew Jaber's conditions were leading to his suicidality. He noted that we relied on an expert who had never seen Jaber.

I responded, "The only reason we do that, of course, is that we have no ability to bring an expert to Guantanamo for an examination. What we address in our papers is that Mr. Mohammed had made quite plain to me that the isolation in which he has lived has been intolerable to him."

"They take the position that those representations about isolation are not accurate," Judge Walton challenged.

We knew this was coming as well. I responded:

> What is not disputed is that, in Camp 5, where Mr. Mohammed has been held, it is not possible to see another human being from one's cell. It is not possible to speak to another human being, except by yelling, but then not if large industrial fans in the corridors are being run. It is not disputed that Mr. Mohammed has only been allowed to have the Qu'ran and letters…it is not disputed that he hasn't had any contact with his family in four years.
>
> What respondents do in attempting to say that he is not held in strict conditions of solitary confinement is make several arguments which I think are very instructive on this point. They say he is not being held in solitary because he is interrogated. He is not being held in solitary because

> he interacts with guards. He is not being held in solitary because he can yell through a food-tray slot in his door, although, again, not if the fans are on. And he is not being held in solitary because he receives, on average, a letter a month.
>
> Those arguments, frankly, I think underscore our point that he is being held under conditions that are quite isolating and that are utterly inappropriate for a man that [the government has] known for years is suicidal.

I was surprised and relieved that Judge Walton let me get all that out. I felt a little more relief when he responded by saying, "I am not unsympathetic to his situation."

But he then expressed concern about becoming "the warden" if he ordered changes for Jaber, noting that no other judge had issued a ruling about conditions. That was true, which made things tough for us in terms of legal arguments. But this was a critical issue. If we could persuade Judge Walton that letting Jaber have books or phone calls wasn't going to interfere with Guantanamo's operations or create security issues, our chances of success had to increase, given that he seemed to understand the human side of the situation. I said:

> What I would point out is that in terms of the relief we are seeking, it all fits within the operational framework at Guantanamo. We are not asking for an end to interrogation, even though that would undoubtedly benefit him. We are not asking for an injunction against abusive treatment generally. We are asking for things that are contemplated by the protective order already entered by the court in this case, and other things that can happen within the framework of Guantanamo as it exists.

I almost wanted Judge Walton to ask more questions about this—and wanting a judge to ask more questions is not always my impulse. But more inquiries might signal an openness on his part to exploring the concrete steps we were asking for and let us provide further assurances.

However, as I finished my pitch on the modesty of what we sought, Judge Walton again raised the issue of whether he had any legal basis to order changes. We had an exchange about the Fifth Amendment, the Eighth Amendment, the All Writs Act, and even the Geneva Convention, which he raised on his own.

Moving on, he asked whether there was evidence to show that if he provided the relief we requested, it could "alter [Jaber's] psychological state" and keep him from being suicidal. I pointed out that our expert said the measures we requested were the minimum that should be done. Also, the government didn't dispute that the steps we wanted taken would help Jaber. I continued:

> In March of last year, I was meeting with Mr. Mohammed. He was describing his conditions, his isolation, and he said to me, "What can I do to keep myself from going crazy?" Naturally, I didn't have a very good answer. . . .

Judge Walton interjected, "And he said that because of his isolation?"

"That's correct. He told me that he had raised that issue with people at Guantanamo before and, obviously, nothing had happened."

Judge Walton said he would hear from the government. I jumped in to raise one more point. I said the government had just reported moving Jaber to Camp 1, but without more detail, we couldn't assess whether that move was meaningful.

One of the government lawyers stood up to offer their side of things. There are lawyers, like Mark, who listen calmly to an adversary's arguments, thoughtfully making notes on a legal pad about points to make in response. I always wanted to be like that. I hope I don't betray how I'm feeling when listening to opposing counsel, but normally I'm not particularly calm. Often I just want to yell back at them after each point. That was especially true here.

The government's lawyer went on about Guantanamo providing great care to Jaber, so there was no risk of irreparable harm to him—again, a point we had to establish. The lawyer also said the government did not contest the proposition that isolation was to blame for Jaber's suicidality, but then went on to claim Jaber had been diagnosed with adjustment disorder with mixed emotional features, a borderline personality disorder, narcissistic personality disorder, and depression. If there was no dispute that isolation was the problem, why bring up these other diagnoses? Just to smear Jaber and confuse the issue, it seemed. Also, if Jaber had all these other conditions, was the government really saying that Camp 5's solid-wall cells had been the right place for him? If he had all these other conditions, wouldn't the need to provide a better environment be even more pronounced?

The lawyer said that in Camp 1, where Jaber had just been moved, the cells were made of steel mesh so detainees could see each other and communicate more easily.

"So, contrary to what [Jaber's] counsel has indicated, he does have adequate opportunity for human interaction . . . the record before you clearly establishes that he is not held under these strict conditions of solitary confinement, especially now in light of the fact that he is held in Camp 1."

It seemed we already had something of a win with the move to Camp 1. But for the government to be crowing about Jaber generally having plenty of interaction based on a move that had just occurred was rich. *Just make a note*, I told myself, trying to stay calm.

The most galling point the lawyer kept coming back to, though, was how there was no risk of irreparable harm to Jaber. I tried to breathe deeply. Finally, I had the chance for rebuttal:

> Mr. Mohammed was probably a couple of minutes from dying when I found him hanging in that cell. The notion that we can't show irreparable harm strikes me as worse than untenable . . . on the point that counsel made that we should continue

> with the status quo and that Guantanamo staff are providing adequate care, those notions are entirely refuted by the fact that Mr. Mohammed, by [the government's] count, has tried to kill himself nine times. . . .
>
> What we are seeking are discrete steps within the framework that exists at Guantanamo to ease the psychological pressure that he is facing. He has said explicitly to me it's the isolation. And whether or not somebody can yell through their tray slot to other people, there is no disputing that in Camp 5, you sit alone in your cell. You can't see anyone. If they turn the fan on, you can't talk to anyone.

Judge Walton asked whether the transfer to Camp 1 addressed these concerns. I said we didn't know the details of Jaber's situation there and that the military could decide to move him back to Camp 5 any time. Judge Walton directed the government to provide a sworn statement about Jaber's specific conditions in Camp 1 within a week. He promised to work on an opinion over Christmas.

That was that. I exhaled. If Judge Walton decided against us, I didn't think it would be because I had fucked up too badly.

Chapter 11

HE'S SUICIDAL BECAUSE OF YOU

While waiting for Judge Walton to rule, we had to focus again on the congressional bill I had told Jaber about. The Detainee Treatment Act (DTA) was being touted as legislation to ensure humane treatment of people held by the military, including at Guantanamo. The problem was it also had language that would throw out everyone's habeas cases in favor of a new process. The new process would allow detainees only to challenge CSRT findings in the DC court of appeals, a much more limited procedure than habeas.

By this stage, there was a big group of lawyers volunteering on the Guantanamo cases. But we were litigators, not lobbyists. Nonetheless, with the help of some established Washington players like Tom Wilner—the cowboy-boot wearing, big-firm lawyer who had been involved with Guantanamo from the start—we mounted a full-scale lobbying effort against the offending part of the bill. I found myself using every connection I could think of to reach the offices of senators and representatives. All of this paid off when the bill was modified so that its language about barring habeas petitions was made to apply to future cases but not existing cases like ours.

On December 30, 2005, President Bush signed that version of the DTA into law. We were in the clear.

It was shocking, therefore, when Judge Walton issued an order on January 4, 2006, saying he had serious questions as to whether the court could exercise jurisdiction over our case in light of the DTA. He gave us eight days to respond. We started putting together a brief to highlight the DTA's specific terms. Then, the day before our deadline and without waiting to hear from us, Judge Walton issued an order staying all habeas cases he had, including ours. That was it. Our motion for Jaber was dead unless it could be revived on appeal, a process that would take forever—or certainly longer than I thought Jaber had.

It's an old adage that you shouldn't take business personally. I never knew quite how to live by that advice and certainly not in a moment like this. Judge Walton had gone out of his way to express sympathy for Jaber. But now, for stated legal reasons that were questionable at best, he had decided not to do anything. Obviously I knew his order wasn't directed at me, but it felt very personal.

I thought about Joe Margulies's approach of using every bad development for some productive purpose. We had to make Judge Walton's decision the next feature of plan B. I wrote a series of emails to Nabeel Rajab that became stories in the Bahraini press. The message was simple: Not only did our clients have to rely entirely on Bahrain to get home, but they would also get no help from US courts while waiting. The *Washington Post* ran a story also, as it continued its coverage of Jaber's saga.

I knew I had to keep up my visits to Guantanamo. It wasn't feasible for Mark to take weeks off from billable work to head to Cuba. But it seemed I had come to an unspoken understanding with the firm that my billable hours would suffer as I put in more and more time on Guantanamo. Or at least that's what I hoped.

For 2005, I missed my billable target of 1,950 hours by more than six hundred hours, which normally would be a quick ticket out the door. But I had put in over 1,100 pro bono hours for a total of about 2,500, so it wasn't like I was relaxing. A number like 2,500 is what was expected of associates for billable work in classic cutthroat New York firms. While fifty hours per week (assuming two weeks' vacation and the other fifty weeks being full-time) may not sound like a ton, it isn't possible to bill fifty hours in fifty clock hours. People need to do things like eat, go to the bathroom, perform the odd administrative task, and just take a break now and then. So, billing fifty hours a week means being in the office closer to fifty-five or sixty hours per week. Billing that amount of time on standard associate work in typical commercial matters would have been worse than professional purgatory to me. But the Guantanamo piece made my overall work pace perfectly good. And so far, nobody had said anything to me about hours, which made me feel lucky—not my normal mindset.

I got approval for a late-January, three-day solo visit to Guantanamo. I was scheduled to see Jaber on each day of my trip, interspersed with visits to other clients. On January 28, I touched down in Guantanamo. At the airport, a military lawyer met me, which was never a good sign.

"I wanted to let you know that we've revised your schedule."

"How?" I asked, immediately tensing up.

"You'll be seeing 361 only one day."

The military didn't use names. They used internment serial numbers, or ISNs. I had learned long before that saying "Jaber Mohammed" on the base would draw only blank stares, so I had adopted the ISN approach.

"Why? I always see him several days in a row."

"There are people here who don't think you should see him at all. You're lucky to be getting one day."

"Who doesn't think I should see him?"

"Some people feel that way."

"You won't tell me who?"

"No."

"Well, then tell me why they think I shouldn't see him."

"Because your visits make him suicidal."

"I make him suicidal? You guys said he tried to kill himself seven times before I even met him. How do you explain that? He's been in isolation for nearly two years. What exactly do you think that does to people?"

I wasn't yelling, but there was no way I could hide my agitation. Based on his name patch, this lawyer was Italian American. Being entirely Italian American myself, his ethnicity made me all the more aggravated somehow.

"I need to talk to someone about this," I said as calmly as I could.

"There's nobody for you to talk to. The decision has been made. If your client stops trying to hurt himself, he might be able to see you more."

"Are you serious? Are you really saying that someone who is suicidal gets to see his lawyer less?" My voice was raised.

The problem—and you can be sure the military knew this—was I had no leverage at all. Our judge had told us effectively that he wouldn't even listen to any requests we made. He wasn't about to direct the military to give me several days with Jaber rather than one. We had no other option.

"Pathetic," I said, walking away.

Now I would have to tell Jaber that the court couldn't be bothered to help him, and I couldn't manage to arrange more than a one-day visit.

The next morning at the Detainee Acute Care Unit, the guards searched me and Abdul, who now was my regular interpreter, from head to toe. Then, they wheeled in Jaber. He had fewer bruises on his body than in November and his facial paralysis seemed to have improved. Otherwise he looked as bad as before—exhaustion and desperation etched on his face. He tried to smile but didn't quite manage it.

I told him, as gently as I could, about the DTA, the court's decision in his case, and my limited visiting hours. Feeling like I had to stop throwing gasoline on the fire, I also said that those things didn't matter so much because our focus should be on the Bahraini government, not Congress, the courts, or the military. Diplomatic pressure would get him home, just like the three clients who had left. I promised Jaber that we were bearing down on the government in Bahrain as hard as we could with help from the press, human rights activists, and parliamentarians. I described every piece of media that had come out in Bahrain about him and our remaining clients just since my November visit. It was a long list.

Jaber hardly acknowledged my words.

I took out copies of letters I had sent him since the November trip to make sure he had received them. He picked one up and began to read it. A guard burst out of the nurses' station and jogged over to us.

"He's not allowed to hold any paper."

This was new.

"He can't hold paper?"

"No, he can look at it, but he can't have it in his hand."

I understood the need for caution, but what exactly could Jaber do with a single sheet of stationery sitting at the table? Even if it could be turned into a deadly weapon, the guards were watching from right across the room.

"What if he needs to write something down?" I asked in a solicitous tone. I knew it wasn't this guy making the rules.

"That's okay. He just can't hold the paper."

If the authorities had decreed that a pen posed no risk, but paper was a hazard, that was the law.

"Got it," I said, knowing this was demoralizing for Jaber.

"Hey, Jaber. Do you remember when I told you that lawyers were boring?"

He almost smiled.

"Why don't I stop talking and let you tell me about what's been happening here."

He spoke slowly and in a near monotone, as Abdul translated for me quietly.

"After you left the last time, the female psych doctor told me that I had to leave the detainee hospital and go to the Delta Block psych ward or Camp 5. Both are isolation. I said I was in isolation for two years and that she knew it was my problem. She said my interrogator wanted me to leave the hospital and so did the head doctor.

"They took me to acute care in Delta Block. There was nobody else in my section. I asked for the female psych doctor. They said she knew I was there and she wasn't coming.

"I covered myself with a sheet on the toilet—they let me do that for privacy. I cut my arm with a razor."

Jaber described falling off the toilet and having what sounded like a seizure. He said a guard nicknamed Smurfette saw him and yelled for help. They took him to the hospital and performed a surgical procedure on his arm.

"I went back to Delta Block in a larger room that had a bed in the middle. They put me in four-point restraints on the bed. I stayed there for four days. A nurse told me the bed was never used for more than a few hours, except for me."

There were marks on Jaber's forehead. He said they were from one of the restraints. After that, he said, the military had taken him to another part of Delta Block.

"There are crazy people yelling all the time there. At least four of them."

"Is anyone normal?" I asked.

"There is a Syrian a few cells away. He takes his medication so you can talk to him. But when I do, they threaten to strap me back to the bed."

Jaber looked inconsolable.

"Imagine that everyone around you is screaming, that you're barely allowed to wear any clothes. Will your situation improve? I am a human being. I want to stop hurting myself, but they aren't helping. I was patient. I waited. I have really collapsed. I don't even care to go home. I swear by God that I will die."

"Jaber, I need you to hang on a little while longer. Your family needs you to hang on a little while longer. Amal needs you."

Was it fair to tell a man in Jaber's circumstances to think about someone else's needs and to invoke his daughter? Maybe not. Or maybe it was what he needed to hear. I didn't know, but I was running out of ways to urge him to stay with us.

"You have to remember you will go home. I can't tell you when it will happen, but it will. You have to remember that being at

Guantanamo is not permanent. It's not like losing a leg. It's not like dying. That's permanent. Those things can't be reversed. But you can leave Guantanamo. In one day, you can fly from Guantanamo to Bahrain or Saudi, and then everything will be different. All of this will be gone forever. These people won't have any more control over you."

Jaber looked down. "I'm very hopeless. I don't know how I haven't gone crazy. I can't take any more pressure. And the government of Bahrain will not do anything."

"They will," I said. "They already brought three people home, and I'm hearing good rumors all the time."

Jaber's voice grew indignant and louder. "One of the Kuwaitis who went home used to fight the IRF team and spray guards with urine. He always called for jihad. A Moroccan who hit soldiers went home. I am still here. I'm not with bin Laden. Zarqawi, I only heard about here.[2] I was never Al Qaeda. I never fought against an American. I never carried weapons."

"I know. That's one of the reasons why you'll go home."

His voice became quiet again. "I thought it would be my turn before, and now I don't even care. Everyone has a limit. I am not considered an animal or even a rock. I live in hell."

I hit my themes again. His family had been through so much. They needed him home alive, not in a box. He had already endured much more time at Guantanamo than he had left to do. Obviously I had no idea if this really was true, and I didn't want to promise things I couldn't deliver, but it seemed a risk worth taking. I pointed out that even though I knew next to nothing about religion, I understood that Islam viewed suicide harshly.

This is how it went for seven straight hours. I offered, restated, and reformulated every argument I could think of as to why Jaber should stay alive. He politely but flatly said none of them was good enough.

A few minutes before I had to leave, we were still at it.

---

2 Abu Musab Al-Zarqawi was an infamous Al Qaeda leader in Iraq after the US invasion.

"Words like 'You will be free soon' are useless and mean nothing," he said. "Please forgive me. My situation is going from bad to worse. I don't need press coverage. I need to rest. You did your job and more. The prisoners tell me my lawyer is taking very good care of me. Thank you. When I hear from you, I see a little light in the darkness, but then the light goes away. I leave Amal in Amir's good hands. Amir should take care of my father and mother."

"Time's up," a guard said, as he and his colleagues filed out of the nurses' station and moved toward us.

I felt despondent. I leaned over and gave Jaber a hug. I whispered into his ear in English. "One more visit. Give me one more visit."

He smiled, but didn't say a word.

Shortly after getting back to New York, I heard from the Privilege Review Team. The PRT was the government unit that assessed whether communications from our clients needed to be maintained as classified. The letter Jaber had given me right before hanging himself in Camp Echo finally had been declassified. The review process took longer than normal because Jaber had put blood on the letter (it was dried when he gave the letter to me), so it was a "biohazard," requiring precautions.

I hardly needed more sobering news, but I clicked on the PDF file as soon as it arrived in my inbox:

Josh . . . I feel very sorry for forcing you to see—it might be the first time in your life—to see a human being who suffered too much dying in front of your eyes. I know it is an awful and horrible scene, but there was no other alternative to make our voice heard by the world from the depths of the detention centers except this way in order for the world to reexamine its standing and for the fair people of America to look again at the situation and try to have a moment of truth with themselves. . . .

When you remember me in my last gasps of life before dying, while my soul is leaving my body to rise to its creator, remember that the world let us and let our case down. Remember that if there were people who are actually fair and who defend justice and defend the victims of injustice, and if there are judges who are fair, I wouldn't have been wrapped in death shrouds now and my family—my father, my mother, my brothers and sisters, and my little daughter—would not have to lose their son forever.

Josh . . . at this moment, I see death looming in front of me while writing this letter. . . . Death has a bad odor that cannot be smelled except by people who are going through the agony of death.

Josh, farewell. Farewell with no hope of your seeing me again. I thank you for everything you have done for me, but I have a final request. Show the world the letters I gave you. Let the world read them. Let the world know the agony of the detainees in Cuba.

Prisoner of Deprivation
Jaber Mohammed
Guantanamo Bay, Cuba
Friday, 10/14/2005

Chapter 12

SWEET DREAMS

Between Jaber's letter and the misery he had exhibited during our prior visit, my only question was when exactly the next bad news would arrive from Guantanamo. In mid-March 2006, a lawyer from a large Manhattan firm who represented detainees called me. She wanted to talk about one of our clients and asked me to come to her office. I understood immediately. A client of hers must have said something about Jaber and the information was still classified. She and I both had security clearances, so we could talk about it alone in a room with closed window shades (seriously), but not on the phone.

I walked to her office with a pit in my stomach. According to her client, Jaber had tried to kill himself again. It was a serious attempt. He had cut his throat and was still in the hospital. It happened on March 11. I felt the familiar combination of numbness and panic.

I wrote to the Department of Justice, asking whether Jaber had hurt himself and about his condition. I didn't expect a response and didn't get one. Having become familiar with the way Guantanamo operated, I called Josh White at the *Washington Post*. He contacted press officers at the base. They wouldn't identify anyone by name but told him a detainee had tried to kill himself on March 11. They also told him that one detainee had tried to kill himself twelve times. I knew the prior Guantanamo count for Jaber's suicide attempts had been eleven, and no other detainee had a number remotely that high. In what was becoming a terrible ritual, I told Jaber's family, the media, and the Bahraini government that Jaber had once again tried to end his life.

There had to be something more to do, even if the courts and the military wouldn't help. Trying to think of any creative and available angles, I wondered about another trip to Bahrain. I regularly wrote to officials there to keep them current on the status of our clients and the litigation. But we hadn't been there in about a year, and it had been five months since our three clients had gone home. We needed to stir that pot directly again. Mark agreed.

We pushed the firm to approve a visit, promising to get a good deal on tickets through Abdullah, whose brother Adel had been released the prior year. Abdullah still worked for British Airways and remained committed to our work. The firm approved. We made reservations quickly, before anyone could reconsider. Chris Karagheuzoff, the colleague who had told me not to "fuck up" before the Judge Walton argument, would come as well.

We sent letters to officials we had met with before at the Bahraini Foreign Ministry and Interior Ministry, asking to visit with them again. We contacted the parliamentarians we had been working with to let them know we would be coming. Of course, we were in touch with Nabeel Rajab, since he would act as general impresario. I arranged to have Jackie Northam, a National Public Radio (NPR) reporter, join us for the trip to ensure we got some coverage in the States in addition to the coverage we would get from the press in Bahrain.

A week before leaving, I heard that the Bahraini government had invited our clients' families for a meeting to discuss the efforts being made to bring people home. We took that as a clear sign that the trip was a good idea.

Nabeel had our itinerary in good shape when we arrived in Manama. We knew the drill after our first trip. Looking over a schedule of events at the hotel on the night we flew in, it seemed as though Nabeel had the right mix of National Assembly members, ministry officials, the media, and client families. I tried to fine-tune the messages I wanted to deliver in each context. Unfortunately, running through things in my head and the unpredictability of jet lag gave me a second wind, despite the fifteen-hour flight. I ended up lying in bed, unable to turn off the spiels I was trying to fine-tune. I finally took some of my red-eye sleep meds to fall asleep.

The next morning, we jumped right into an Amnesty International–sponsored press conference at the Bahrain Bar Association, our old haunt. The room was packed with reporters, family members, human rights activists, and others who were simply interested. I spoke about Jaber's despair and the failed efforts to get the court to help him. Mark and Chris discussed our other two remaining clients. We stressed that the court process was stalled and that hearings for our clients were not even on the horizon. Without the intervention of the Bahraini government, we had to assume our clients would be at Guantanamo forever.

"We know the government of Bahrain understands how serious this is," I said.

The crowd listened intently and asked question after question.

Our next event was a *majlis*. As Nabeel (and the internet) had informed me, a majlis is a sitting room, typically in a home, where people gather to discuss issues and socialize. This one was to be at the house of Sheikh Mohammed Khalid, another parliamentarian. We were told he was a big advocate for our clients. We were told also that he had strict religious views. Someone said, perhaps not in jest, that we shouldn't ask Sheikh Mohammed what he thought should happen to the hands of thieves.

The majlis was attended by other elected officials, the press, families of our clients still at Guantanamo, and two of our released clients, Abdullah and Adel. It was a revelation to see them. We had only ever known Abdullah and Adel in jumpsuits and shackles. Now they were walking around, chatting, smiling, and getting a bite to eat—just like normal people.

I found myself alone with Abdullah at one point. He was the client who had asked with bitter irony if I could get him a clock at Guantanamo—saying, in so many words, that having a lawyer might be useless. I had told him he wouldn't see any benefit from our work until he got off the plane in Bahrain. When I said that, I was both exhausted and desperate to offer some justification for our existence. I had no idea at the time if I was right. As it turned out, I was. At least in his case. Abdullah and I had a quiet moment recalling the exchange.

Jaber's brother Amir was there, as was his uncle, whom I had met on an earlier visit. We hugged. I gave them a brief update, leaving out as much drama as possible. We agreed to talk more later when we weren't in a crowd.

Sheikh Mohammed Khalid convened the group. He thanked us for our work. He said parliament was supporting our clients every way it could and would continue to do that. He opened the floor to us. We talked about the endlessly delayed court case, the hunger strike one client had been on for months, Jaber's hopelessness, and the critical need for Bahrain to act. The parliament members in attendance promised to do even more.

The next day we had a meeting in a large, ornate room at the National Assembly. The foreign minister was there for a time, and the parliamentarians pressed him on the slow pace of negotiations, pointing out that our released clients were doing well, and our detained clients, such as Jaber, were doing terribly. The foreign minister said he and others were moving "not slowly or pleasantly" to resolve the situation.

Someone suggested drafting a petition that all members of parliament in Bahrain would sign. The petition then would be delivered to the US Congress, including copies hand-delivered to specific influential representatives. That sounded like great ally-to-ally communication. We talked about which members of Congress would be the best recipients, focusing on people who were security-minded but not fanatical.

The Interior Ministry was our next stop and quite instructive. We learned the Bahrainis were surveilling our three released clients to placate the US embassy, which had asked whether those clients were being watched. Officials told us they hoped this would improve the chances of getting our other clients home by showing the Bahrainis could be relied on from a security perspective. Indeed, the Bahraini government had "held" the three returning clients for two hours upon their arrival just so the US could claim it had transferred them to Bahraini custody rather than releasing them outright. This was theater, but whatever statecraft got people home was fine with us.

We also spent hours that day with the families of the clients still at Guantanamo. I had a long talk with Amir, Jaber's brother. I wanted to project calmness, but Amir obviously knew Jaber was in desperate straits. So I spoke honestly, even if leaving out some of the more hellacious details about Jaber's self-harm.

Amir gave me family updates that I could pass on to Jaber. He said Jaber's daughter, Amal, was doing well in sixth grade. She often drew pictures of Jaber. Amir was switching jobs. One of their sisters was working on her master's degree in education. A brother was working at a car dealership. I could imagine Jaber smiling as he heard these pieces of news—or at least there was a time when he would have smiled.

Hoping to spark something of that feeling in Jaber again, I asked Amir to arrange for the family to write long personal letters to him. I said the letters should have plenty of detail about people's day-to-day lives. I thought that orienting letters to quotidian events, in addition to whatever expressions of love people wanted to send, would help ground Jaber. It might help him focus at least a bit on the tangible parts of life beyond Guantanamo. A life I had promised he was going back to with as much conviction as possible.

We could send the letters to Jaber in Guantanamo through official channels, which were always slow. I wasn't allowed to hand the letters to Jaber, but thanks to a quirk in security procedures, I could jot down their content and read that to him as long as it didn't contain prohibited information.

Our last full day in Bahrain involved a series of meetings at the Ministries of Justice, Interior, and Foreign Affairs. At each stop, we offered our gratitude for Bahrain having brought back three of our clients. There was no reason not to give credit where due for that. Otherwise it was repeating talking points we could offer in our sleep: The US courts were moving at a glacial pace; Jaber was suicidal and we had no way to help him; another client was alive only because of nasal feeding; the US government would not transfer anyone unless it felt pressure; and clearly it was up to Bahrain to continue to bring pressure to bear, given the prior transfers of our clients. Official after official promised the Bahrainis would do everything they could. We said we had no doubt about that and that we had assured our clients this would be the case. We repeated those sentiments to the local press covering the visit. Shortly after the trip, Jackie Northam did a series of reports on NPR as well.

The military had approved a Guantanamo trip for May 2006, shortly after we got back from Bahrain. A few days before I left, a DOJ lawyer told me a client letter had arrived at the secure facility. I asked the Privilege Review Team to determine whether it could be unclassified. The next day, a copy of the letter arrived via email. It was Jaber's first English-language letter to me. The date was March 8, just three days before the March 11 suicide attempt I had heard about from the other firm:

My dear friend Josh. Finally I found a good chance. Finally I will get my freedom very very soon. When you receive this letter I will be done. I will not going to suffere to eny abuse from now on. How wonderful the freedom. Finally. I am so happy now. by the way I just sent you this letter to inform you that's it also is to late to eny thing for me now. enyway thank you Josh about evry thing, you did for my.

Jaber

I felt the beginning of an instinctive surge of panic but tamped it down by telling myself that Jaber was alive and I'd be seeing him soon.

My colleague Lauren Rasmus was going to come with me to Guantanamo on the May trip. I thought that one of our clients might object to meeting with a woman, but Lauren had done a lot of work on the case and it seemed right to give it a shot. Plus, I knew Guantanamo had special meaning for her since her dad had served there. As it turned out, Captain Ron Rasmus (ret.) had become a huge supporter of our work, which I was particularly grateful for given his long naval career. And I knew I didn't have to worry about Jaber objecting to a female attorney. To be honest, part of me dreaded seeing Jaber given his state, so the idea of company was appealing.

Outside the DACU before we met with Jaber, the guards seemed to have gotten a new memo about suspicious items carried by lawyers. Lauren had migraine medication in her bag, and I had an EpiPen, a vestigial item from an allergic reaction to a sting years earlier. The EpiPen had never been a problem before at Guantanamo, but now it was contraband along with Lauren's medication. We weren't allowed to bring either in. I didn't remotely care about leaving that stuff outside, but losing time from our meeting to deal with it was very frustrating.

When we finally got into the DACU, Jaber was sitting there in his wheelchair with the usual entourage of guards, medical staff, and shackles. At least it was usual to me, but I thought Lauren registered a bit of shock at how Jaber was being handled.

Jaber said he was able to walk, but someone had decided wheeling him around was easier logistically, so the chair had become a fixture. We hugged. His bones seemed to protrude through his skin. I introduced him to Lauren and asked if he minded her being there. He smiled at me as if I should have known he would be fine with it. Seeing him a little animated was great. It also made me realize I could read his moods from the briefest expression—I guess we were in a type of long-term relationship where that happens. I then saw a two-inch scar stretching across Jaber's Adam's apple.

I decided to do everything possible to keep the conversation away from the misery of Guantanamo, at least initially. Talking about that had not been a winning formula lately.

Right away, I said, "Jaber, get comfortable. Get something to eat," pointing to the food Lauren and I had put on the table. "I have a lot to say."

He seemed agreeable, immediately grabbing some M&Ms and a meatless Egg McMuffin we had just picked up at McDonald's. As usual, he mostly ignored the culturally appropriate, high-end Middle Eastern food we had lugged from New York.

For the next two hours I barely took a breath while detailing everything we had done since my prior visit in January. I told Jaber about the Bahrain trip, repeating several times every encouraging utterance we'd heard from Bahraini officials. I described the nineteen stories about him and our other clients that had appeared in the Bahraini press during the prior few months. I said I had gotten our released client, Abdullah, interviewed on *This American Life* to humanize people who had been at Guantanamo. I had told Jaber's story for the same episode. Also, I had arranged for Abdullah and Adel, another released client, to be on NPR during our trip to Bahrain. There were articles in the *New York Times* about hunger strikes that described the experiences of another client of ours who had been force-fed.

I told Jaber about bringing Adel's brother Abdullah (of British Airways fame) to a conference on Guantanamo at the George Washington University, which was broadcast on C-SPAN. Adel spoke about the effects of Guantanamo on his brother, and I told Jaber's story. After the conference, I heard from Tony Ricci, my former Kosovo colleague who had been the first to tell me a plane had hit the Twin Towers on 9/11. Tony now worked on detainee issues at the Pentagon—not that he agreed with how they handled everything. Tony said his office had tuned into the conference.

"You're doing great advocating for your clients," he told me. "You're definitely making a lot of noise."

I had thought about the "noise" angle. We were never going to convince a majority of the American public to sympathize with our clients. But still, there was some domestic cost to the government when it was forced to deal with Guantanamo news. If a disproportionate amount of news was being generated in connection with one or two detainees, would that encourage the government to transfer those people, particularly if the government didn't think they really were bad guys? My unscientific sense was that the government did see value in sending someone home if it would cause an outsized reduction in "noise." At least, that theory was part of plan B.

I told Jaber about Tony's comment, omitting identifying information, of course. I also described interviews I had done about Jaber on CNN and the BBC, as well as three additional *Washington Post* articles that had come out. I promised we were doing everything we could to spread the word.

I then turned to the family letters from Amir. Parts of them sounded like the kind of stuff I might have expected my family to write if I had been in Jaber's shoes.

Jaber's mother penned a heartfelt letter, but at the end she changed tone in a way Jaber often did, writing, "Listen, this is a joke for you. A man tells his wife to heat up water. The man's friend tells him, 'Yes, that is how a man gives orders and shows his authority.' The man replies, 'Well, am I supposed to do the dishes in cold water?'"

I had laughed when I first read it, and we laughed now as I read it to Jaber. Not exactly the humor I had anticipated from an older Saudi woman.

One of Jaber's brothers wrote about his anger at Jaber's imprisonment, but he also said that he planned to buy a car for Jaber. "Don't worry," the letter went, "I am not going to buy you a crappy 1983 Mitsubishi Galant like the one you had before. And do you remember the car Amir had that was as old as Noah's ark?"

Jaber loved the letters and wanted to hear them several times.

"Why do they keep teasing me about that car?" he asked, laughing.

I didn't know if it was the letters or the magic of my whirlwind recitation of events, but Jaber's mood was different from what it had been on my prior three visits. He was engaged. He ate. He was the old Jaber at least for the moment. It dawned on me that although my cheerleading probably didn't hurt, Jaber had seemed better from almost the moment we walked in.

"I'm optimistic, by God's will," he said shortly after I had finished reading the letters.

That morning he had dreamed about going home. The dream was a message from Allah to be patient, he told us by way of explanation. In fact, he had been dreaming about being with his family for a while. He took all of that as signs.

Also, a Kuwaiti detainee told Jaber that his lawyer had said the Kuwaitis and Bahrainis would be released soon. I thought it was unlikely that Tom Wilner and the other lawyers for the Kuwaitis would make an unconditional promise like that, but I let it go. Frankly I didn't care what gave Jaber a little hope if it wasn't entirely delusional. It was May 2006, and for the first time since July 2005, I felt relaxed talking with him.

"Wait a minute, Jaber," I said. "You just let me go on and on about everything instead of just saying you're feeling good?"

He laughed.

Of course, we were still sitting at Guantanamo, not poolside somewhere, so our conversation turned grim at times, including when Jaber described the March 11 suicide attempt.

"That day, I felt really, really sad and desperate. I was isolated. I couldn't continue. At eight o'clock, during dinner, I took the lid off a yogurt container. I rolled it up and reached through the food-tray slot in the door. The keyhole in the door is big, and I stuffed the lid into the hole. I pushed it in too far to be pulled out.

"I waited until eleven o'clock, when the guards eat dinner. I was shaking. I knew they wouldn't be able to save me. When I had tried to kill myself before, I knew there was a chance for them to save me. This time I thought it was for sure or I wouldn't have done it because they make too much trouble for you if you survive.

"I had a razor blade and used it to cut the vein on my leg." Jaber showed us a long, deep scar that seemed to be healing on the inside of his thigh.

"While I was cutting, a soldier came by. She saw me and yelled, '361 bleeding. Snowball, snowball!'"

By now, I understood that "snowball" was the code for a suicide attempt.

"I kept cutting. I hit the vein. It was like a fountain. The SOG [Sergeant of the Guard] and guards came. They couldn't open the door. They yelled for me to stop.

"I had planned to cut my left and right legs and arms, but when they came, I didn't have time. I went to the mirror and covered my head with a sheet, so I didn't have to see them yelling 'stop.' I looked into the mirror and cut my neck. Blood came shooting out. The room was covered with blood. It was like a horror movie. I was screaming and falling and standing. I was hysterical. I couldn't focus. I couldn't cut anything more. I was semiconscious."

Jaber told us what he remembered about the guards finally getting into the cell and taking him to the hospital, where he had surgery. He said that for the next two months, the military kept him tied to a bed.

It was gruesome.

I quickly glanced at Lauren whose pen seemed to be pushing hard into her pad as she took notes. To her credit, she kept her expression calm. I didn't want Jaber to see either of us react with the shock I felt and suspected Lauren did also. He didn't need more drama. As I asked follow-up questions, we maintained an air of concerned calm as best we could. After a while, the discussion moved on.

I mentioned that I had been sure Jaber would not object to meeting with Lauren. I kidded him that I had almost expected him to throw me out so he could finally enjoy the company of someone else. He laughed and talked about the fact that some detainees refused to have women attorneys.

"You know," he said, "I have told detainees with female lawyers, 'Just say thank you.' She's not asking for money. They say it doesn't create a good image to have women support them. I say it's not enough to have God defend you."

Jaber thanked Lauren for wearing a hijab to cover her head but said it wasn't necessary.

We spent our standard seven hours together. At times we laughed, and at other times Jaber became very serious. This had been our pattern during my first visits to Guantanamo. It was tough but not unremitting, and there was humor. Jaber poked fun at me for being too serious, which Lauren especially enjoyed.

"You'll never get married if you're like that," he joked.

We had a few minutes left when I asked if Jaber wanted me to say anything to his family.

"My family shouldn't worry about me. I have no thought to hurt myself again. I have hope that I will see my family again. My dreams mean that I will see them."

It was the last thing I expected to hear when we walked in that morning.

That evening, Lauren and I were at a picnic table outside the Combined Bachelor's Quarters, our home away from home. It wasn't uncommon to see other habeas lawyers there, and often there was a group barbeque. After a day interviewing clients, I usually just wanted to take a run around the Leeward side and head to my room for a sandwich from the Subway on the Windward side. That was a substandard meal compared to what people were eating outside in the Caribbean night air, but I typically didn't have energy left for socializing. This was Lauren's first trip, though, so I thought it better to step up.

A lawyer from another firm came out with a six-pack. The three of us had a beer and chatted. Minutes later, a young woman joined us. She didn't look like a military contractor, so I took her for a habeas lawyer I hadn't met; the CBQ didn't get much traffic from other people. But then she introduced herself as a journalist named Emily Witt. That was unusual. As I understood it, the military housed reporters visiting Guantanamo on the Windward side of the base, across the bay from where we stayed. I figured that was to keep them away from the lawyers. Maybe the press officers got confused booking accommodations in this instance. Regardless, it was a chance to evangelize about Guantanamo to someone with a platform. I turned the conversation toward the detention operation.

Back in my room later that evening, I wondered if I had gone on too long. Sometimes I even bored myself with my shtick. I also thought about whether I had revealed anything our clients had just told us. That information hadn't been declassified, and disclosing it would violate a bunch of laws. I couldn't think of anything through a slight Red-Stripe haze.

Three weeks later, I was flipping through the *Village Voice*, waiting to meet someone for dinner. There was "Pearl of the Antilles," a story by Emily Witt. I thought she wrote for a paper in Miami, but evidently that paper had some connection to the *Voice*. The article said:

> On May 11, a trio of attorneys gathers there [at the Combined Bachelor Quarters, or CBQ] with six-packs of Red Stripe and bags of snack food. . . . One is a measured sort, not quick to pronounce her opinions. Another is even quieter. He seems more comfortable discussing his upcoming wedding than the legal labyrinth of Guantanamo. And then there is Joshua Colangelo-Bryan. A brown-eyed, affable attorney on his seventh visit to Guantanamo, Colangelo-Bryan is a native of New York City who lives in Brooklyn. . . . Colangelo-Bryan has traveled to detainees' homes in the Middle East and met with their families. And he's not publicity shy—on his last trip to Bahrain, an NPR reporter accompanied him; he has interviewed with everyone from *Harper's* to *New York* magazine; and there's even an entry under his name on Wikipedia. Moral outrage comes easily to him. He can muster it even after a sunset swim at the leeward side's tiny beach.

The piece went on to cover a good number of my usual talking points: We had clients not even accused of acting against the US; the Administrative Review Boards our clients went through at Guantanamo could recommend holding someone based solely on a statement extracted through torture; and, legally speaking, you can't have a "war" against a tactic such as terrorism. The article also covered Jaber's story in some detail. It seemed like my usual shpiel had worked well enough.

An immutable rule I took from Guantanamo, and perhaps life generally, is not to get too comfortable. On June 10, I received an email from Carol Rosenberg, a journalist then with the *Miami Herald* who has covered Guantanamo more exhaustively than anyone else. She told me the military was reporting the deaths of three detainees by suicide and asked if I knew about it. For a second, I froze. Just as quickly, I felt sure it wasn't Jaber, not after our last visit. It was spooky how sure I felt. Later that day, the military disclosed that two of the detainees had been Saudi (the government always treated Jaber as Bahraini) and one was Yemeni.

I was seething nonetheless. For months we had shouted from rooftops that when you lock up people in isolation, without charge and potentially forever, at least some will become hopeless. It was inevitable that people would try to kill themselves. Feeding my anger, Admiral Harry B. Harris, Jr., who ran the detention operation, told the press that the suicides were "asymmetrical warfare." A State Department spokesperson opined that the deaths were "good PR" for the detainees. These were not the government's first attempts to disguise reality through perverse framing, having previously referred to suicide attempts as "manipulative self-injurious behavior" or "hanging gestures" and calling hunger strikes "voluntary fasts."

I needed to respond. As I had come to be seen as the suicide expert by reporters covering Guantanamo, I went on CNN and *Good Morning America* to talk about Jaber and the hopelessness of indefinite detention. *ABC News* came to our carriage house on Sunday morning to do an interview, with a staffer trying to make it look like an office by putting books on a ledge behind my chair. The Sunday *New York Times* did a piece. On Monday, I went to Washington, DC, for a press conference about the deaths.

The next week, a long story came out in *New York* magazine, titled "The Minutes of the Guantánamo Bay Bar Association," a moniker some had started using to refer to the habeas lawyers, at times in good humor, at times mockingly. Stacy Sullivan had written the article months earlier, but it was edited to focus on Jaber and published at that point because of the deaths. Stacy was the author of a book about a Brooklyn roofer who supplied arms to fighters in Kosovo, so we had a lot of common ground. *New York* magazine asked a group of lawyers from the original New York habeas firms to go to a photoshoot for the piece. Nine of us arrived at a building in downtown Manhattan and were led into a bare basement room that had a long table and, yes, a bare light bulb hanging down. I couldn't decide if it was completely glamorous or just tacky. Either way, the article was excellent. Obviously we didn't have any power to change Guantanamo directly, but carrying out plan B was better than sitting around feeling powerless and angry.

Not that this press activity didn't have its dangers even beyond getting nasty voicemails or hearing how a client of the firm was upset. At a partners' meeting held shortly after this batch of stories came out, one partner opined that I was out of control in the media and just generating press for my own glory. He said I couldn't be trusted and should be fired. Cooler heads prevailed and nobody else signed off. I would have been very upset if I had known about this in real time. But when I heard about it off the record, the issue was settled. That didn't keep me from playing out scenarios in my head about what I would do if, say, I was told not to do media (a rule some habeas firms had) or got fired. In my mind, at least, I responded with a passionate "fuck off" and kept doing what I thought I had to. It's easy to be bold in your mind.

As I calmed down, I tried to reflect on whether I was getting seduced by the media attention. I knew there was ego gratification in getting quoted by a prominent news source. But I didn't think there was a way *not* to have those feelings while serving as our clients' voice to the world through the press, a role I believed was critical. All I could do was resolve again to make the story about the clients, and not me.

The end of June 2006 saw another big development. The Supreme Court issued a decision in *Hamdan v. Rumsfeld*, a case about criminal trials at Guantanamo. Criminal trials were not an issue for anyone other than the handful of people who had been charged. However, in *Hamdan*, the Supreme Court rejected a government argument that the Detainee Treatment Act barred consideration of existing cases brought by detainees; this was the issue Judge Walton had raised to avoid ruling on our motion for Jaber. In our view, the language of the DTA was clear from the beginning that the law had no effect on pending cases. *Hamdan* confirmed that. But it also underscored that Judge Walton perhaps just preferred to avoid ruling on our motion, since plainly the DTA did not compel him to abstain. In turn, that underscored our need to work plan B even harder.

Thankfully we also got some remarkable, if cryptic, news about the potential effects of those efforts. An Agence France Presse (AFP) story appeared, quoting an unnamed diplomat of an unnamed country who said a deal had been struck to bring our three remaining clients home. One would leave first and then two more subsequently, it said. We didn't know how AFP got this story or who the source could have been, but the news was reported in fairly definite terms. It was tantalizing information.

I called a Bahraini reporter who covered Guantanamo. The reporter had already spoken to a Bahraini Foreign Ministry representative after seeing the story. The representative wouldn't comment on the record because the topic was so sensitive, but had said, "It looks very positive for all three."

Chapter 13

KEEPING THE PEACE

If anything, the urgency of plan B very quickly became starker. Jaber's brother Amir called me. His voice wavered as he told me their father had just succumbed to cancer. I knew he had been sick, but not that sick. It wasn't a topic Jaber brought up much, so I had not focused on it, given the number of grim issues we had no choice but to discuss. I told Amir how sorry I was in that inadequate way you do in those situations. We decided this was not news I should give Jaber or that the family should share with him in letters. Jaber was in such a precarious place and wouldn't have the support necessary to deal with it. I ran this news-blackout approach by Mark, Chris, and Lauren, who all agreed. We would do nothing.

On July 6, the Privilege Review Team sent us a letter Jaber had written in mid-June that had just been declassified. In his letter, which was dated June 8, Jaber wrote that two psychiatrists and the Guantanamo "cultural advisor" had come to see him. They told him his father had died. With a formality that most client letters had when translated from Arabic, Jaber wrote:

I was so overwhelmed by the news that I fell ill, especially that the news came during extremely adverse conditions. I have none of my things, and

I am still in solitary. . . . My psychological state worsened very much lately, made worse by the sadness over the death of my father, may God bless his soul. . . . I do not think that I will carry on much further. I feel very unwell, and I feel that my end is imminent. Please, if you can, come and visit me in Cuba, even without an interpreter, very soon. Do something for me. I am almost in the throes of death.

I was stunned. This was a person who struggled to hold on to his will to live under what passed for normal conditions at Guantanamo. It was a detention operation where the government said nobody had any rights and certainly no right to family information. Letters clients received from their own children were frequently redacted to the point of incoherence. But somehow the government decided Jaber absolutely needed to know his father died. And as messengers, they chose military staff Jaber didn't believe cared for him at all. That included the "cultural advisor," a Muslim man and native Arabic speaker whose job was to address "cultural" issues in an appropriate way, but who was viewed by most detainees as just another member of the detention staff.

In a near rage, I wrote to the Bahraini Ministry of Foreign Affairs. I spoke to parliamentarians, including Sheikh Adel, who promised to raise the issue in Bahrain. At the same time, I gave an update to various Bahraini journalists to ensure the story was covered. All of us working on Jaber's case joined to send him a letter of sympathy. We stressed the various steps we were taking in response. This had become standard practice after any bad news.

We wrote to the Department of Justice, asking what the hell the military was doing, albeit in more professional terms. We asked that Jaber be allowed to call home, a request we had originally made after the October 2005 suicide attempt. We asked that I be allowed to move up a visit scheduled for late August. And we asked that the family letters I had brought for Jaber during my May visit finally be delivered to him, since as far as we knew, that hadn't happened.

The Bahraini Foreign Ministry responded quickly. I took their alacrity as a small triumph. The Ministry said it would coordinate a delegation visit to Guantanamo. Recalling our clients' descriptions of harsh questioning from Ministry of Interior personnel on prior delegation visits, I made a mental note to ask the Bahrainis to take a more sympathetic approach this time. The Foreign Ministry said also that the Bahraini embassy in DC had officially requested improvements to Jaber's living conditions. And the Bahraini ambassador was working to get a family call scheduled for Jaber. It was as much as we could expect from the Bahrainis.

The military did not expedite my trip, so I arrived at the base on August 14, with meetings scheduled for the following three days with Jaber as well as Salah and Isa, our other remaining clients. When I sat down with Jaber the following afternoon, I touched his arm and told him how sad I had been to hear about his father. He smiled but didn't say much. It looked like he wasn't ready to talk about that—or anything else—yet.

I decided to jump in to fill the space. After putting food on the table, I did my usual routine of repeating everything from the letters I had sent since our prior visit and supplementing with new information. Normally I focused on family news first. I wondered if that was the wrong approach now but decided to follow the usual drill. It's not like we could pretend nothing had happened by ignoring family news, and maybe some lighter family information could still be comforting.

Using Amir's phrase, I told Jaber there was "this guy from the Mohammed tribe," a very distant relative perhaps, interested in marrying Jaber's youngest sister. Amir and another brother had been checking him out and he seemed acceptable. This guy's family had visited the prior week to discuss marriage, but nobody wanted a ceremony before Jaber got home. And the suitor wanted Jaber's approval.

I told Jaber that his daughter was on summer break and visiting his mom most days. I said that Lauren from my office sent her best.

"She says you're lucky you don't have to share the baklava with her this time."

A small smile.

"Let me tell you what I'm hearing about people getting out of here," I said. That might resonate more.

I told Jaber about the Agence France Presse story that had described an unnamed diplomat as saying there was an agreement to bring the three Bahrainis home. I reported that I had spoken to a Bahraini journalist who was told by a Foreign Ministry representative that "It looks very positive for all three."

"This is a big deal, Jaber," I said. "I realize the article isn't specific about when, but it's clear that things are developing. Good things are happening."

He did not contest the point. Nor did he seem animated by it.

I moved on to the correspondence we had been exchanging with the Bahraini government. Two days earlier, I had learned the Bahrainis were approved for a delegation visit to Guantanamo in September, and they were promising it would be purely a supportive trip. The Bahraini parliament had delivered its petition to the US Congress. I told Jaber about a large demonstration that had been held at the biggest mosque in Bahrain. There had been fifteen articles in the Bahraini press, almost all based on emails I had sent to Nabeel Rajab for dissemination to journalists.

Truth be told, I had gotten a little obsessive about placing stories in Bahrain. A seemingly insatiable desire for Guantanamo news had developed there, so any absence of coverage could be cured by my providing additional material. If two days went by without a story, I began to feel like I was falling down on the job. After three days, I would get a gnawing anxiety and had to come up with the elements of another piece to send.

One of the Bahraini news stories had quoted the Bahraini Foreign Minister saying that Guantanamo was a "serious blight" on Bahrain's relationship with the US. Another quoted the US ambassador in Bahrain saying he wanted the situation "resolved" and that he had invited Bahraini officials to the US for further talks. I told Jaber this was consistent with the information we had been getting unofficially about increased efforts.

I also told him about an op-ed by Ana Menendez in the *Miami Herald*, titled "It's Time to Close Guantanamo, Mr. President." It recounted Jaber's story before noting that President Bush himself claimed he wanted to end the detention operation and concluding, "Well, then do it, Mr. President."

"Jaber, I have to say I'd had a couple of drinks when I talked to the writer who did that piece about you. I'm glad I didn't say anything crazy."

I hadn't planned on mentioning this, but it came out instinctively.

Jaber, a teetotaler as a devout Muslim, laughed. "You're talking about me when you're drunk?" he asked.

"Not drunk. Do you know the word *buzzed*?"

That summer and the summer before, in 2005, I had gone to a retreat held in Minneapolis for summer associates from all the firm's offices. Summers associates (or "summers") were law students who spent a couple of months with the firm in between school years. The firm tried to impress them, including by bringing them together for a few days that mixed just a little business with lots of wining and dining.

That year, I had spoken to the summers after a panel that included Walter Mondale, who was senior counsel at the firm, and Alan Page, a judge and NFL Hall of Famer. I apologized about how rapidly the speakers' qualifications were plummeting from session to session. But many summers were enthusiastic about pro bono work, and the firm wanted to tout the kind of cases they could do. I was a great example for that, even if it was left unsaid that nobody else put in anything approaching the pro bono time I did. I was happy to help with the messaging, though, particularly because it meant the powers that be saw recruiting value to the Guantanamo work.

After my talk, the group decamped to a fancy boat docked on the Mississippi for more revelry. The bar area was packed, with plenty of actual lawyers from the firm in attendance, both associates and partners. After two vodka tonics on an empty stomach, I felt nicely relaxed.

My phone rang. It was Ana Menendez from the *Herald*. I didn't know if I could talk with the kind of precision I normally aimed for but figured it was worth a shot. By that point, I could recite our clients' stories in my sleep, particularly Jaber's. The resulting article hit the nail on the head.

After laughing about my being "buzzed," Jaber warmed up a bit, even if just to talk about hard things. He reported that there had been a general clampdown since the three suicides in June. Guards were tougher. Nice ones, including one he called "Pee Wee," were transferred off the blocks. Also, as I had heard earlier from our client, Isa, the use of Immediate Response Forces was increasing.

Jaber said the military continued to hold him in the horribly misnamed "Mental Health Unit" (MHU). The primary form of mental health care came courtesy of "psychtechs" who visited the detainees' cells to ask formulaically, "Are you sleeping well? Are you eating? Are you having thoughts of harming yourself? Are you having thoughts of harming others?"

In the MHU, the lights in and outside Jaber's cell were off at night. The air conditioning was set very high.

"It's like being in a hole in a mountain of snow and ice," he said.

Eventually, Jaber spoke about his father. He had been at rec when the two psychiatrists and cultural advisor came to him. The advisor said they had "bad news" and told Jaber that there had been a story of his father's passing on the internet. Jaber was informed that the "Admiral"—presumably Admiral Harris, who called the three suicides "asymmetrical warfare"—had approved a phone call home. Jaber said he did not have words to describe how he felt when he heard about his father's death. After rec that day, he vomited.

The Red Cross visited Jaber not long after. A representative said the organization had contacted his mother after learning of his father's death. His mother had been clear that she did not want Jaber to be told about what had happened, which the Red Cross communicated to the military.

But as I had heard from Amir before coming to the base, Jaber did get a ten-minute call with the family. Jaber told me he had been accompanied by a doctor and an interpreter. He said his mother talked first. There was crying and brief reminiscing about a few old family stories. Amir had described going to the American embassy in Bahrain for the call, and that two Americans were in room for the whole thing, observing with severe expressions on their faces.

I was trying to figure out how to raise Jaber's spirits when he told me about a dream he'd had a few days earlier. In the dream, he was going to leave Guantanamo within two weeks. I had no idea where these dreams kept coming from and was sure the two-week timeframe was not realistic, but I was prepared to ride the optimism of Jaber's dreams for all it was worth.

"That's terrific," I said. "Soon your dreams and your actual departure will match perfectly."

Maybe it was thinking of the dream, but Jaber's mood brightened. Jaber said he had seen his old interrogator, Jeremiah, in passing.

"Do you remember him?" he asked.

"Don't punk me, motherfucker, you know where I'm from!" I responded, cracking both of us up. "Yeah, I see that guy in Brooklyn all the time," I continued.

Jaber mentioned that some of the guards had started to take notice of the attention his case was getting in the press. They had said they knew he would write a book when he got home. "Don't write about me," one had told him in good humor. Another had taught Jaber to say, "Same shit, different day."

At one point in our conversation, Jaber shifted to geopolitics. I had to be especially careful because lawyers were prohibited from providing any information about current events to clients. Mostly I was left reacting to what Jaber said without adding anything.

Jaber talked about groups that he said harm Islam by using the religion to justify wrongful actions. He pointed to Saddam Hussein, saying that when Hussein was in trouble during the 1991 Gulf War, he claimed to be fighting Israel. And he mentioned the Pakistani security services that had helped to build the Taliban to serve their own purposes. I almost said something about Hussein getting tried by a court in Iraq at that time but caught myself.

Defying all my expectations, at the end of our meeting, Jaber said not to worry about him.

"I won't try to hurt myself. It only makes things worse," he told me.

Perhaps seeing that my expression was still concerned, Jaber said in a singsong voice, "Don't worry, be happy."

For once I felt better when I got home from Guantanamo than when I flew down there. But there was work to do. Or, more accurately, there was some of the billable work that always needed doing, ultimately in the amount of 1,250 hours that year in addition to 1,000 Guantanamo hours. Mark and I were defending a Chilean investment firm accused of getting a married Chilean couple into risky—and losing—stock and bond positions. The case was in New York because the investment contract specified that disputes be resolved there, even though nobody could remember why it said that.

Perhaps obvious to say, my usual sympathies tend toward the underdog. But it was hard to decide who the underdog was in this case. The couple had a patrician air and were older. Old enough so that if you did the math, it was clear they fared well during the Pinochet regime. Also, they were of German extraction, and although we didn't know if they had alighted to Chile after World War II, those demographics raised a red flag in my mind. Maybe more to the point, the evidence showed the husband drove the investment strategy, even directing the firm to buy him "when and if" bonds from Russia in the late 1990s. As I learned, these bonds would have had a great return if they paid, but that was an entirely speculative proposition. The bonds ended up close to worthless, and the husband—who had lied to his wife about the investments—sued.

I was reminded of a case I had done several years earlier in which a couple raising a disabled son accused a large financial services company of exercising total control over and abusing their investment account. My initial sympathies lay with the couple. But the evidence showed that the husband—an able-bodied guy who scammed the New York Police Department out of a disability pension—was day-trading speculative tech stocks. Also, in attempting to prove the broker had complete control over their account and lives generally, the couple testified that the broker not only picked a specialized school for their child but also the "shrubbery" they planted in their yard. What credibility the two might have had disappeared after that testimony. We prevailed on every aspect of that case.

The Chilean matter wasn't scheduled for trial until the following spring, but there were depositions to take and motions to make. While all of that required close attention, it also provided a little psychological breathing room from the life-and-death feel of Guantanamo. Unsurprisingly, Guantanamo kept the breathing room minimal.

Congress was demanding our time once more, in this instance because elected officials were agitating to overturn the *Hamdan* decision. Again, in *Hamdan*, the Supreme Court had interpreted the Detainee Treatment Act's provisions that invalidated habeas cases as not applying to cases filed *before* the DTA's enactment. Now, our clients' many political opponents were working on a bill called the Military Commissions Act (MCA) that would explicitly provide that even habeas cases *already* filed had to be thrown out in favor of the limited review process created by the DTA.

Adding to the madness, the MCA would create rules for the small handful of detainees who were or would be charged with crimes. The reputed worst of that group, including the alleged mastermind of 9/11, Khalid Sheikh Mohammed, had arrived at Guantanamo from secret CIA detention facilities just a couple of months earlier, in the summer of 2006. The purpose of that transfer, in part, was so the Bush administration could argue there were serious bad guys at Guantanamo in pushing for the MCA. The criminal-trial rules in the MCA weren't great, but they provided far more process than one would get through the DTA procedures that were to replace habeas. As a result, someone charged with killing thousands on 9/11 would get a better chance to prove his innocence than someone never charged with anything.

We had to lobby hard against the MCA. In a coordinated effort, the habeas lawyers contacted every representative and senator who might have even a touch of sympathy for the rule of law. Suggestions were made about how the bill could be modified to do away with the habeas-related provisions. Arguments were made on legal, ethical, and practical bases. I wrote a letter, signed by over five hundred New York lawyers, that we sent to New York's senators and congressional representatives, protesting the bill.

It was an uphill fight. Elected officials were decidedly unconcerned about getting voted out of office or losing campaign contributions due to being "tough" on terrorism. Rather, many were more than happy to campaign specifically on being "tough," which really meant opposing anything that could benefit anyone at Guantanamo, regardless of the legal or national security consequences. Nobody saw political upside in coming out for due process; those who planned to oppose the MCA, I'm sure, did it for principle rather than calculated political effect. And the conventional wisdom about what played with ordinary Americans was undoubtedly correct, given opinion polls still showed most people were happy to let detainees rot.

So, I was hardly feeling optimistic when a DOJ lawyer emailed me on October 16, 2006. I opened the message, bracing for bad news. Instead, it read, "I am writing to inform you that petitioner Salah Abdul Rasool Al Bloushi (ISN 227) has been released from United States' custody and transferred to the government of Bahrain."

I read it several times to make sure I wasn't having some sort of delusional episode. It was almost exactly a year since our first batch of clients went home. Now Salah would be joining them. In truth, he should have been the first person to leave Guantanamo—out of just about everyone ever there. Mark had fittingly described him to a crowd in Bahrain earlier that year as a "gentle soul who loved soccer and wanted to be a teacher."

I called Salah's father, who always greeted me warmly with a personalized salutation of "Hello, Mr. Young Man." During every single phone call and meeting we had had over the prior two years, I had heard acute fear and anguish in his voice. During those conversations, I hadn't been able to do much more than say that Salah was alive and looked as healthy as could be expected. Now I could tell him his son was coming home. The relief and elation in his voice were palpable. I said he would have to get Salah into the gym to bench press with him soon.

I shook my head looking again at the part of the DOJ email talking about a transfer "to the government of Bahrain." I remembered the Bahraini officials who said they were happy to hold people for an hour or so upon arrival just so the US could make that dumb point about a transfer instead of admitting a release.

I took a few minutes right then to exult in our achievement. Plan B was working. But the very next day, President Bush signed the MCA into law. We knew that soon the government would ask the court to dismiss all habeas petitions. And this time they would have a statute whose language required dismissal. I did some rough calculations as to how long we might have left on the case and wondered whether the government would start trying to restrict our access to the base.

Next, I got fresh stories in the Bahraini press, explaining how the government would try to throw us out of court and prevent Jaber and Isa, our other remaining client, from ever getting fair hearings. We wrote to the Bahraini government making the same points and reiterating that our clients desperately needed their help. Articles about the MCA came out in the *Christian Science Monitor*, the *New York Times*, and the *Washington Post* with my comments about the law's cruel ironies. Thankfully I didn't hear rumblings about any renewed effort to have me canned.

Three weeks later, in November 2006, I was in Guantanamo to see Jaber and Isa. I had spoken in English with Isa from the start, and Jaber's English had gotten pretty good. So, for the first time, I went to the base without an interpreter.

As I walked into the Detainee Acute Care Unit to meet with Jaber, I saw him at our usual table, playing cards with a psychtech and a couple of guards. That was a first. It looked like blackjack. After the psychtech and guards moved to the enclosed nurses' station to keep watch over us, Jaber said the card game was solely for my benefit, just to show me they were caring for him. I hoped that wasn't true.

As always, I was worried about Jaber's level of despair, particularly because I didn't know how he felt about another client going home without him. After laying out the buffet, I went right into my rundown of recent events, putting the most positive spin on things that I thought my credibility could withstand.

Jaber knew Salah had left, but I highlighted Bahraini press articles reporting that the foreign minister attributed the release to the king, the prime minister, and the crown prince—the three most powerful figures in Bahrain. The foreign minister also was quoted as saying officials were working harder than ever with the US to "close the files" of all Bahrainis. In another article, the foreign minister said the Bahrainis were having extensive contact with US officials to bring people home.

I reminded Jaber of an Agence France Presse story we had discussed during our prior visit in July. That piece had quoted an anonymous diplomat who said there was a deal to bring home all three Bahrainis, with one leaving first and the others after. So far, we were on track with that.

Jaber did not seem particularly moved by my reporting on release-related issues, so I tried family news next. I told him that Amal was studying hard, doing her best to get good grades. Arabic was her favorite subject. Amir also was working hard, with a one-hour commute each way to his job and a shift from 7:00 a.m. to 7:00 p.m. I told Jaber that Amir had requested some good news from Jaber. Jaber didn't offer anything up in the moment.

Only after trying to prime the pump with positive developments did I raise the MCA. I explained that the government would try to end our case. I didn't say that I feared the government might soon try to keep us from getting to Guantanamo. And I reminded Jaber with as much bravado as I could muster that we didn't really care what happened in court. That's not how four of our people had gotten out of Guantanamo and that's not how he and Isa would go home.

"I can tell you more about the new law," I said. "But, you know, same shit, different day."

Jaber laughed. He didn't seem worried about the MCA. And he seemed in relatively good spirits again. Once more, at least part of the reason was his dreams. He said that most nights he dreamed about sitting and having long talks with his father. Sometimes, after these dreams, he found himself thinking he would see his father when he went home. I understood him to mean that this was comforting, not sad.

To be clear, Jaber wasn't saying that his day-to-day had improved. For a time, he had been allowed to go to rec in the Mental Health Unit with a detainee known as Abu Bakr with whom he was friendly. More recently, though, he was being sent to rec with a Yemeni man who had been brought to live in the cell next to his. This man believed—sincerely, it appeared—that he was Jesus Christ. He ranted day and night about being the savior. Jaber's problem with the Yemeni wasn't theological but just that living next to and going outside with a crazy person made him feel crazy and hopeless. A psychiatrist had told Jaber that he would stay in the MHU for as long as he was in Cuba. I could barely imagine surviving a night in that environment, which sounded like a perfect setting for a nightmare.

On the other hand, the Guantanamo library lending policies seemed to have improved. Jaber had finished a Harry Potter book and now had a copy of *Anna Karenina* in Arabic and English. I remembered getting rejected when I tried to send *Beauty and the Beast* in English and Arabic, and Judge Walton not even ruling on our request for dual-language books. I also regretted not having read much fiction since college and having never read *Anna Karenina*. Jaber had to carry the book club discussion about *Harry Potter* and *Anna Karenina*.

Evidently tiring of shouldering that burden alone, he asked, "Are you married yet?"

That wasn't surprising since he asked me to explain my lack of a legally binding romance as often as my grandmother did.

"What, you think I got married since my last visit and didn't tell you?"

"It's time for you to get married."

"I know . . . but . . . it can be hard to find the right person." I winced at telling Jaber that anything on the outside was "hard."

Jaber wasn't interested in my equivocation. "I know you. You don't buy the cow because you get free milk," he said, grinning.

"I don't buy what? Where did you hear that?"

Jaber had learned it from a guard who said he didn't want to get married.

"Did I use it correctly?" Jaber asked.

"Yeah," I laughed, "you did, but no, it's not about free milk. I just want to make the right decision."

Jaber waved his hand at me with playful dismissiveness. "Maybe you'll be married in the next life."

Chapter 14

CONNECTIONS

While I didn't want to ignore Jaber's admonitions about matrimony, there was a Chilean investment matter to contend with back in New York and more work to do with Congress. Even after the MCA passed, we kept at it, advocating for an amendment to the statute that would remove the habeas-stripping provisions. On one of several trips to DC, I sat in a quiet corner of the Capitol building with Gabby Giffords, who had just been elected as a representative from Arizona. She was thoughtful about the issues and seemed to have true empathy for the human side of things. In fact, she offered to lend some staff time to organize talks on Guantanamo I would give in Arizona. It struck me as remarkable for a new representative who was not exactly representing Berkeley, California.

Others were not so welcoming. A few of us met with a senior aide to Senator Joe Lieberman. He assured us that the senator's grasp of national security issues was so advanced and nuanced that our input was scarcely of note. It took a lot of self-control not to point out that the senator, in his vast wisdom, had been a huge champion of the disastrous Iraq War. Ultimately it wasn't surprising that the MCA's habeas provisions remained on the books.

I was more determined than ever to visit the base often and in short predictable intervals. I planned my next trip for mid-January 2007. Just a few days before I was heading to Guantanamo, my office phone rang. My secretary yelled to me, saying there was a doctor on the phone. Had I forgotten I was expecting test results? Was it good news or bad news if the doctor called to deliver them? Mildly confused, I picked up.

A male voice said, "Hi, I was a doctor at Guantanamo."

If this was legitimate, the chance to talk to someone who had been on the inside was beyond rare. My mind started racing about how to handle it.

The caller gave a first name, saying he didn't want to disclose his last name. I can't be sure if he gave me his real first name, but I'll call him "Jim."

Jim said he met Jaber during a tour he had served in Guantanamo. Jim told me he had been reading about Jaber in the press, which prompted him to get in touch. Jim told me he saw Jaber on most of his days in Guantanamo and found him smart and likeable. He would seek out Jaber just to say hello because he enjoyed their conversations. He reported that he and Jaber would tell one another jokes and that Jaber enjoyed translating for medical personnel.

I said I could imagine Jaber enjoying that kind of human interaction and remarked on how comfortable it had been for me to talk to Jaber from the start. Jim said he never felt in danger at Guantanamo, including when he was in prisoners' cells or sitting on a detainee's hospital bed. There were some bad people, he figured, but most of the detainees were "regular guys" he couldn't help feeling empathy for.

I mentioned how hard it had been for Jaber in Camp 5, given the isolation. Jim understood and told me I had a tough job. "When Jaber's down, he's really down and doesn't want to talk to anyone." I knew what he meant.

After talking a bit more, Jim said he needed to go. As we exchanged goodbyes, Jim said, "Tell Jaber that his 'root beer friend' says 'Hi.'"

I knew Jaber was going to love hearing that Jim had reached out. On another occasion, I had gotten a phone call from someone who knew Jaber during a brief period he spent in Bloomington, Indiana. She had gone to the same mosque he had. She remembered Jaber leading Friday prayers in a routine, apolitical way. But she remembered him best because he played with her young kids. She recalled a time when a mosque elder had yelled at her son for running around, but Jaber said they should just keep playing.

When I had told Jaber about the phone call with the woman from Bloomington, he lit up. I could see how touched he was that she had reached out to say nice things about him and wish him well. That human connection and kindness, even conveyed through me, meant so much to him.

Another time, I had gotten an email from someone who said she was a Catholic nun. She wrote that she had started a hunger strike in solidarity with the detainees. Jaber was very moved. "Remember the nun?" he asked from time to time. The same was true of a sympathetic woman from France whose letter to him had somehow made it through the Guantanamo censors. All of it just underscored how truly social he was.

About seventy-two hours after my call with Jim, I was sitting in the Detainee Acute Care Unit, waiting for Jaber. Guards wheeled him in. His hands were cuffed in front of him, attached to a metal block that sat by his waist. His legs were shackled with padded ankle cuffs I hadn't seen before. And guards had put big headphones and blackened goggles on him. His body was tiny. He almost didn't look human.

The guards took off the goggles and headphones so at least I could see Jaber's face. They said the cuffs were going to stay on his hands, which wasn't a surprise. The padded ankle cuffs that secured Jaber's legs kept him from moving them at all. I shook my head and asked the guards if this was truly necessary. They told me they had already asked for permission to remove the ankle cuffs, but their request was denied. After a little discussion, it was agreed that Jaber could lie down on a hospital bed that was wheeled over. At least he would be able to stretch out a bit. This was a bad way to start a meeting. I worried Jaber would be in a desperate state of mind, even without the excessive shackling.

After Jaber was carried onto the bed, he and I figured out a way that I could hand him food. His appetite seemed reasonable. That was a good sign.

I told Jaber that one of his sisters was pregnant and feeling fine. Amir was working on the construction of new petrochemical plant. Jaber's mom had just come back from visiting his youngest sister in Bahrain. And his daughter Amal was taking exams that week. She had decided that history and Arabic were now her favorite classes.

We ran through the press coverage before focusing on the most interesting article I had seen since my last visit. It was a *New York Times* piece reporting that Bahrain and Kuwait had been pushing the US to send people home, regardless of whether the Administrative Review Boards at Guantanamo recommended release or not. This was another good sign, I told Jaber.

Without dwelling too much on any of that, I told Jaber about the call I had gotten from the former Guantanamo doctor. I thought this would give him a boost.

Jaber smiled, immediately remembering his "root beer" friend. "He was a good guy. He brought food and asked what people needed."

Jaber said he was grateful that the "root beer doctor" had reached out. "Remember the nun?" he then asked.

Jaber's description of life on the Mental Health Unit never sounded good. His friend Abu Bakr had been moved to the far end of the block, and it was hard to communicate with him now even by yelling. On the other hand, at the request of staff, Jaber had convinced Abu Bakr to go to rec, which Abu Bakr had been resisting. As a reward, Jaber was allowed to go to rec with Abu Bakr instead of with the Yemeni who thought he was Jesus. Jaber said he and Abu Bakr played chess there. Abu Bakr's wrist was so small he could reach through his caged enclosure into Jaber's to move his pieces.

In a more intriguing development, Jaber said he had been called to a meeting with a woman who wore civilian clothes and said she was from the US embassy in Bahrain. She asked Jaber how he was doing. When he told her about the MHU and the lack of medical treatment he could trust, she replied that she was sorry to hear that.

"It was not an interrogation," Jaber said. Obviously he would know.

The woman told him the Bahraini government was working as hard to bring him home as it had with the four Bahrainis who had already returned. She told him she would be meeting with the Bahraini foreign minister. She also said that she knew other things that she couldn't say.

"What do you think about all that?" I asked him. Nothing like this had happened before.

"I think it was real," he said. "I don't think the MHU would let a pretend meeting happen. And a corpsman was there. Corpsmen can't go to interrogations."

I had never known that rule, but I agreed that this didn't seem like a ruse. I couldn't imagine what the point would have been to go through that kind of charade. It sounded like good news.

Jaber also said a guard had overheard a doctor saying something about how "the governments are working hard to get 361 home." When quoting staff, Jaber often just used his internment serial number as the staff did. It seemed that the net effect of this information had Jaber in a pretty good place. He said nothing about hurting himself. He didn't return to the topic of his living conditions.

The guards and other staff I saw generally looked to be in their late teens or early twenties. As Jaber told it, that's often how they acted, but sometimes to an extreme. He had seen a female guard perversely nicknamed "Snow White" flashing her breasts to a crazy detainee one night. She always spoke to Jaber in breathy, seductive tones. One time she said she had watched a detainee do "number three."

Jaber's American slang stumped me. I knew number one and number two, at least as far as being code for going to the bathroom. But number three?

"What's number three?" I had to ask.

He looked at me like I was a step slow. With a somewhat embarrassed expression on his face, he said, "You know . . . like . . . jerk off."

"They must have come up with that after I was a kid," I offered to explain my ignorance.

Another guard had said to Jaber, "I'll give it to anyone who wants my dick. Ugly, fugly, pretty, I don't care."

"Is *fugly* really a word?" Jaber wanted to know.

"Only in that expression," I told him.

"I know your family is looking for a wife for you, but you're never getting married if you keep learning English like that," I said. "Do you ever learn anything polite?"

Jaber tried a few out: "It's not you who decides what will happen"; "Let's get something straight"; "What if I don't care?"; and "You're talking to the wrong person."

It sounded like he'd been speaking to the world's strictest camp counselor, which probably was the most charitable spin you could put on his best interactions with the military.

Moving to more erudite subjects, Jaber gave me a lesson in religious studies. He explained that Judaism, Christianity, and Islam all look to the same God, an idea I had never contemplated before.

"Some people say 'Allah,' some say 'God,' but it is one supreme being," he said. "God sends prophets when people forget his rules. God made people with needs, so they are different from God. Each religion has a complete book from God: from Moses for Jews; the Prophet Mohammed, peace be upon him, for Muslims; and Jesus for Christians."

Jaber also explained that the origin of the Sunni-Shia split was a disagreement about who would be the successor to Prophet Mohammed. I would have done some homework if I had known this discussion was coming. I was very light on theology and couldn't be sure if Jaber was entirely accurate, but it certainly seemed like a reasonable, balanced presentation.

At the end of the visit, we had a warm but casual goodbye. I was bowled over by Jaber's continued resilience. I barely needed to encourage him. It was much more like hanging out than the amateur therapy sessions from a year earlier.

Back in the office, there was a lot of litigation going on. Mark and I had the trial in our Chilean case coming up in front of Justice Ira Gammerman. If you asked central casting for an irascible, sharp, grizzled New York judge, Justice Gammerman would be first on the list. It was a wonder they didn't have him hearing arraignments on *Law & Order*. Our case was going to be a bench trial, meaning Justice Gammerman would play the fact-finder role that a jury typically does.

The plaintiffs, again, were a wife and husband. Interestingly, the wife—who had seemed a reluctant participant in the case before—now was fully onboard with her husband's theory that they were financial neophytes who had been preyed upon by financial professionals. In trying to support the theory, she answered questions differently on cross-examination at trial from how she had answered during her deposition. The problem, for her, was that I had her deposition transcript in my hand for the cross-examination and just kept pointing out the discrepancies. This pattern persisted for a while before Justice Gammerman signaled he'd heard enough. The conventional wisdom was that it took just a minute or two for Justice Gammerman to decide if someone was playing fast and loose with the facts, and after that, his mind was made up. Nothing else the plaintiffs did went much better, and we got a complete defense verdict.

In an immeasurably more important case, we got a terrible result. The federal appeals court in Washington, DC, had been contemplating the government's motion to dismiss the habeas cases. That motion had been filed after the MCA passed and was based on the law's clear statement that habeas cases had to be dismissed. Our side had argued that the US Constitution provided a right to habeas that couldn't just be stripped by the MCA. The DC appeals court had been very inhospitable to detainees throughout the litigation, so it was not shocking that it ruled against us. But it still was an awful result.

Without habeas, a detainee had no way to make the government prove he was an "enemy combatant" before locking him up forever. The chance to present evidence to counter the government's arguments would disappear. Effectively, the government would be able to hold people as long as it wanted without presenting a legitimate justification to a real fact finder.

More holistically, we were facing a scenario in which the DC appeals court—generally considered second in authority only to the Supreme Court—had blessed a law passed by a majority of the Congress and signed by the president that rightly should have been considered unconstitutional. It put in stark relief once more the forces arrayed against us.

Of course, we had long ago discounted the chance of a fair hearing in favor of our plan B, which was working. But even that incremental progress was cold comfort. The government had been hinting that if the habeas cases were dismissed, it would restrict attorney access to the base. It was frightening to think what that might do to Jaber personally as well as to our general strategy, which obviously relied on getting information from clients and broadcasting it.

The one litigation option now was to ask the Supreme Court to hear the case. In the 2004 *Rasul* opinion that allowed detainees to bring habeas petitions, the Supreme Court had reversed a decision by the DC appeals court. So, there was a chance. But the Supreme Court hears only a small handful of cases presented to it, and even if it does, you still have to win. Not good odds.

In early April 2007, I was in Guantanamo for a one-day visit. It was all I could fit in, given the press of other work.

At the Detainee Acute Care Unit, Jaber greeted me with "Your Majesty." I thanked him for offering the appropriate salutation.

As I put pastry and chips on the table, he pretended to look in my food bag and asked hopefully, "Cheesecake?" I had written him that I would bring Junior's cheesecake, a Brooklyn staple that had become one of his favorites. I pulled the cake out next.

No matter how many times I offered fruit, nuts, or anything else that didn't have sugar as its main ingredient, Jaber went straight for the sweets. I couldn't blame him. Later that day, there was a chocolate bar on the table he hadn't touched. It was obvious he was waiting for me to have first dibs. I told him to take it.

"You're right," he said. "You're free."

"I just hope you brush your teeth sometime soon," I said, feeling the film on my teeth from the sweets I hadn't been able to resist.

Jaber wasn't concerned about dental hygiene. "When we're ninety, we will blend baklava and drink it together," he said.

I told Jaber that his daughter had done well on the exams she had been taking during our prior visit. His pregnant sister found out she was having a girl and was still feeling pretty good. And, as Amir had said to me, I told Jaber that the "big people and little people" in the family were sending their love.

I reported on the press we had seen over the prior few months. I described a few talks I had given. Summoning my game face, I told him about the DC circuit court's decision in the MCA case, immediately saying it didn't really matter since our path home wasn't through the courts.

"Also, we're asking the Supreme Court to step in," I said. "The Supreme Court has only had good rulings for detainees so far."

Jaber seemed eager to move on, which was fine with me. The month before, he said, a Bahraini delegation had visited. They told him to stay "calm" and that they were "working for" him. One of them said, "Our visit is a very good sign, as you will see when we receive you at airport in Bahrain."

I was practically jumping up and down. "That's awesome! Did any delegation ever say anything like that to you before?"

"No," he said, smiling.

The delegation told him that Bahraini officials had been putting tremendous pressure on the US embassy in Bahrain, which had led the embassy to send someone to see him. That confirmed that the visit from the American "embassy" person had been legitimate, as we thought. Jaber also reported that delegation members asked whether he would live in Saudi or Bahrain after his release. He had said Bahrain, believing it might be the delegation's preferred response.

I had given this some thought. Jaber had Bahraini and Saudi citizenship. He was traveling on his Bahraini passport when the Pakistanis grabbed him, so he was considered Bahraini at Guantanamo. That seemed like the preferred designation, particularly because of the way our Bahrainis had been going home.

But there might be advantages to seeking release as a Saudi. More of Jaber's family was in Saudi than in Bahrain. The Saudis had set up a significant rehabilitation program designed to help people transition back to normal life. In Bahrain, by contrast, people got a physical at the airport and then were largely left to their own devices. Someone like Jaber would surely benefit from more comprehensive care. Also, based on things I was hearing from Amir and elsewhere, the Saudis were providing some financial support and help getting jobs for those who came back.

As a practical matter, this question of home country didn't change our approach. It wasn't as if we could go to Saudi and rile up the media and the parliament, since there was no free press and no parliament there. We probably wouldn't even get entry visas. So, focusing on Bahrain was the best practical option.

Amid all the talk about going home, Jaber was still stuck in Guantanamo. He said that an Algerian with shrapnel in his head was housed nearby and laughed "like the devil all night." Jaber had ear plugs for a while, but they had been taken for some reason. A sergeant of the guard called "Cueball" had taken the Algerian's comfort items for four days after the Algerian stripped naked in rec.

"He is not normal," Jaber said. "They should be more patient."

Making things worse, Jaber's friend Abu Bakr had been moved farther down the block during the first day of the Bahraini delegation's visit. When Jaber walked by Abu Bakr's new cell later that day, Abu Bakr said he had been IRF'd during the move. Jaber asked to talk to the SOG about the IRF and Abu Bakr's being farther away. In response, a guard threatened to have Jaber IRF'd. "If you act like a child, we will treat you like a child and use force," the guard said. Jaber was still traumatized by the IRF beating meted out to him in Camp Echo years earlier. He said nothing more to the guard, but clearly he was feeling his isolation acutely again.

"I can't talk to Abu Bakr because he's on the other end of the block and doesn't hear well. I have no one to talk to. I can't tell day from night. I feel finished. Sometimes I don't have anything to keep me going."

"What will you do when you go home?" I asked, trying to shift his gaze beyond Guantanamo.

"I can't think about that," he replied. "I am only thinking about how miserable life will be in a few hours when you leave and I go back to Mental Health."

I reminded him of everything the delegation had said, the positive stories we were seeing in the press, and that four of our six people had left. It was just a matter of time for him. His mood didn't seem to change.

"The Red Cross visits me sometimes," he said. "They told me the 'general' didn't want to let me go because it would encourage others."

It took a minute for me to figure this out. It sounded like a conversation that had happened closer to the October 2005 suicide attempt when General Hood was in charge. It was Admiral Harris who ran things now.

"Fuck whatever the general said," I told Jaber. "The decisions about you going home are not made by the general or the admiral. Those decisions aren't made by anyone at Guantanamo. We're talking about high-level stuff. Like the king and the president."

I heard myself using a tone of utter certitude. I hoped it was warranted.

Lunchtime was approaching. Jaber needed to go to the bathroom. I had to find a microwave for some frozen shrimp scampi I had gotten at Jaber's request from the NEX supermarket in downtown Guantanamo.

The galley—which is what everyone called the cafeteria—in the hospital had a microwave. As I was leaving the galley, enjoying the fragrant aroma of microwaved shrimp, a TV tuned to Fox News caught my eye. The news ticker at the bottom of the screen said that the Supreme Court had refused a request to hear a Guantanamo case. The only Guantanamo-related request in the Supreme Court at that time was our request for a review of the DC appeals decision that had tossed our cases. Now we knew the Supreme Court wasn't interested either. If I had walked out twenty seconds earlier, I could have remained blissfully ignorant of this latest broadside—at least for the rest of my afternoon with Jaber.

Heading back to the Detainee Acute Care Unit, I briefly considered if I should tell Jaber about this. Quickly I dismissed the thought. He couldn't do anything with the information except feel lousy. I would just go back to my game face, and we would talk about anything but the case.

We managed to have a decent afternoon, largely free of doom and gloom. It really was amazing to see Jaber keep battling with his hopelessness and mostly winning. But in the back of my mind, I knew we were living on borrowed time and that Jaber could not survive just sitting in his cell forever.

Chapter 15

CODE BLACK

On May 10, 2007, I thought we might have run out of time. The Privilege Review Team sent us a letter that day that it had just declassified. Jaber had written it on April 18, 2007, not long after my prior visit. In the formal tones that client letters had, it began:

I do not know how to start my letter. Misfortunes have become unbearable, disasters increased, catastrophes have heavy hands on me, doors have closed, all roads are blocked, earth with all its spaciousness seems much smaller to us, our souls constrained by the small space we live in. . . . I can say that life and death, here in Cuba, are equal, but death has become my greatest hope to end the misery and suffering.

Jaber wrote about recent episodes with IRF teams in the Mental Health Unit:

I'm physically tired to a degree I have never reached before because of the IRF soldiers storming cells and generating sounds to terrify us. Add to that the screams of the prisoners as a result of the assaults. This reminds me of the torture I faced before.

It sounded as though his normal living conditions had deteriorated as well:

I have been sleeping on the cement floor and have nothing to cover my body except my pants and an orange shirt. . . . We are treated here as if we were animals. However, I think I have overstated that. Animals enjoy life and are better than us one hundred times. What kind of creatures are we?

Jaber wrote that he actually had *requested* an interrogation in the hope it might result in some improvement. Apparently his request went nowhere. He wrote, "They don't care about someone who has no information and wants only to complain about great oppression."

The letter concluded with Jaber saying:

I want to put an end to this psychological and physical torture by any means. . . . It is easy for you to say be patient since you eat the best food, wear the best clothes, sleep on the best beds, do whatever you want, say whatever you wish, go wherever you choose, watch whatever you like, and own whatever you prefer. Simply, you are a human being. But for me, I own nothing: no food, no clothes, no time to sleep . . . nothing at all. At any moment, they take my clothes off and leave me naked. My greatest wish is a heart failure after which they can do whatever they want with my body.

I wrote to Jaber the next day, knowing it had been several weeks since he had sent his letter and would probably be several more before he got mine. I said I understood how easy it was for me to ask him to be patient and that it really was an enormous request. But, desperately hoping I was correct, I said that his situation, while horrific, was temporary. He would get home. "You will again be able to eat what you want, wear what you want, see who you want, and do what you want," I wrote. I told him I had a visit planned for June, realizing that could sound like an eternity even if it might be May when my letter arrived.

Guantanamo soon generated more bad news. First, the Department of Justice told us it planned to allow us a total of three more visits to the base, given that our habeas cases were done and we could proceed only under the Detainee Treatment Act. In the government's view, the DTA allowed for such a limited process that a lawyer would not need much time with a client to prepare. Second, there were reports of more hunger strikes. Then, on May 30, the military informed the press that a Saudi had died of suicide, the fourth such death. Since Jaber had never been considered a Saudi there, I didn't believe it was him (although I thought of the man's family immediately). But conditions always got worse after events like this, and I was sure Jaber's would too.

More plan B was the only option. I did the usual writing of letters to the Bahraini government and generating stories for the Bahraini press. The *New York Times*, *Los Angeles Times*, and *Guardian* soon had articles about the Saudi's death in which I was able to get bits of Jaber's story. I spent three days in Arizona doing Guantanamo talks at churches, synagogues, and other spaces, including through coordination with Gabby Giffords's great staff. It was way better than doing nothing.

My trip to the base was scheduled for June 27, 2007. A few days before heading out, I was tidying up other matters. In the back of my mind, I thought about how Jaber's remarkable run of relative optimism seemed to be running out. I tried to think of what I might be able to tell him to revive that feeling just a little.

The phone rang. It was our released client Abdullah, whose family was well connected in Bahrain. He had heard that Jaber and Isa would be home by Ramadan, which was going to be in September that year.

"Tell them it will definitely happen," he said to me. "Tell them not to do anything to jeopardize it."

My pulse quickened and I grabbed a pad to try to get down his exact words. I wanted details, of course, but I didn't want Abdullah to feel like I was pressuring him. Also, it wasn't as if Abdullah would have seen some written agreement between Bahrain and the US or some other ironclad documentary proof of release dates. This information by its nature was going to be a bit amorphous.

On June 28, I was in Guantanamo for the twelfth time. I gave Jaber a quick family update and then launched directly into the news from Abdullah, figuring that was the only thing that might land with him. I said to Jaber also that there had been somewhat vague references to similar timeframes here and there in the Bahraini press.

"You know that they never give timeframes," I said, perhaps making things sound a little more definitive than I believed they were. "It's a very good sign that they are now. And just think about everything else we've heard from the Bahrainis over the past six months that has been generally positive about negotiations." I ran through a catalog of statements.

He wasn't buying it. "If the government really cared about its people, it would say very firmly to the US, 'Give us Jaber' after the first death or after the last death at Guantanamo. But they don't care. What do they lose by letting me stay here? Nothing."

"That's not true," I countered. "We know that they're feeling pressure about Guantanamo. That's how Abdullah and Salman and Adel and Salah went home." I emphasized each name to get as much rhetorical value as I could.

"They went home because the Bahraini government felt it had to do something and it did. The government will do the same for you, and they basically are saying publicly that it will happen before Ramadan."

"I know a lot of people feel humanely about our case and that we should be treated better," Jaber said, "but it doesn't help because I am still here alone for three years in isolation. I am destroyed. I am alone. I cannot even read the Qu'ran sometimes. I just cry."

As I feared, the military had quickly clamped down even more on the Mental Health Unit after the suicide in May. Jaber wasn't going to rec with Abu Bakr anymore, and they still were kept at opposite ends of the block. Jaber suspected that his rec time with Abu Bakr had been curtailed because the psychiatrists thought he would encourage Abu Bakr to hurt himself. Really, he said, it was just the opposite. If he and Abu Bakr could spend time together, they would both feel better.

Jaber told me that his isolation and loneliness made him scared of everything. At night, he lay in his bed crying, too anxious to sleep. He heard scary music in his ears. He heard voices. His request for Ambien was denied. When he managed to fall asleep during the day, guards made noise or banged on his cell door, waking him up.

He blamed much of this on a new head nurse in the MHU, who went by "Brick Red." According to guards, she even had ordered that the detainees' meals be made smaller.

"I don't want to do anything," he said to me, "but how long can I handle this?"

Jaber had put that question to one of the psychiatrists. She told him the camp commander had ordered everyone in the MHU to go to recreation alone and she couldn't change it. A guard told Jaber that the military just cared about keeping the detainees alive and would put them in a freezer until they went home if it were possible. "Nobody wants to cure you. Nobody cares about you," he said.

I got a small taste of this when Jaber asked to use the bathroom. Guards came over to remove one set of shackles, attach another, and walk Jaber to the bathroom. During the process, one of them barked, "361, stand up! 361, walk straight ahead!" He probably thought nothing of his commands, but it seemed like the worst way to treat a small, compliant, suicidal man who was surrounded by burly guards. I wanted to say something but knew it would only make things worse for Jaber later.

His mood was no better when he came back from the bathroom.

"I am social," he said. "I cannot be alone. I told the doctor, 'Be warned. Don't say 361 didn't talk to you or tell you what's wrong.' She said, 'I know, I know.'"

He continued, "I think about how awful it would be for my mom to wait for six years and then get my body back. But I am in a corner. I cannot be like this."

Since our May 2006 visit, when Jaber had rediscovered some hope, I had been dreading this reversion to desperation. I was about to trumpet again the fact that the Bahrainis had promised to bring Jaber and Isa home, when the loudspeaker crackled.

"Code black, code black. This is not a drill. All MAs to Quarter Master Deck."

Guards sprang out of the nurses' station saying they had orders "to remove 361." Jaber and I barely could say goodbye, but I was able to remind him that I had permission for a two-day visit, so I hoped to see him the next day. Really, I prayed I would see him the next day.

My escort and I took the elevator downstairs. As we got out, a woman who looked like a doctor was saying, "It's ugly, you don't want to see it" to a few other people. I heard someone say something about setting up a "perimeter."

We were about to walk out of the building when a hospital official stopped us, saying, "We're in lockdown. There's no movement."

A minute later, my escort talked to another officer to see if we might get permission to leave.

"Are you connected to the package?" the officer asked. The "package," a "perimeter," "code black"—it felt like a Bruce Willis movie.

My escort said we didn't know anything about the "package," which certainly was true for me. The officer let us leave.

In the parking lot, I asked, "What are the odds someone will tell me what that was all about?"

"Not good," the escort said.

"Can you tell me what an 'MA' is?"

"Master-at-arms" was the reply. I learned later that MAs are security specialists in the navy.

I knew any requests for information would be fruitless. Using my time-tested approach, I called a reporter and told her what had happened. She talked to someone at Guantanamo, who said there had been a bomb scare. A bomb scare at Guantanamo? It seemed unlikely, but so did a lot of things that happened there.

The next day, to my surprise, the military let me see Jaber again. His mood hadn't changed.

Jaber said he had needed the bathroom after getting back to his cell the day before. "There's a new rule," a guard had told him. "You only get thirty squares of TP at once."

I knew Jaber's emotional state was such that any slight would be devastating. Saying he could only have thirty squares of toilet paper would more than qualify.

I also noticed that Jaber looked uncomfortable. He grimaced and tugged at the bottom of his shirt.

"What's going on?" I asked, sitting up so I could see better.

There were dark red stains on Jaber's shirt and pants. *Oh, fuck*, I thought, feeling a familiar combination of panic and resignation.

Jaber explained. "When I got back from our meeting yesterday, I had no comb or TP. The SOG said, 'New rules.' I hit the door. I was very mad. The nurse gave me Ativan to calm down.

"After three hours, I went to the shower area that has a toilet. I sat on the toilet backward so nobody could see what I was doing. I started cutting my stomach where there is a huge artery. It hurt a lot because what I had was not sharp. It took thirty minutes. There was a lot of blood. I reached the artery. I was going to cut more, but touching made it feel like fire. I fainted. I felt very bad when I couldn't cut the artery because I knew I was alive and they would torment me."

"What did you use to cut yourself?" I asked as calmly as I could. Really, I was just buying time as I tried to figure out the best way to handle this.

"A piece of metal. It wasn't sharp so it took a long time. While I cut, I flushed the toilet so the guards thought I was using it."

"Did they give you medical treatment?"

"The guards were there when I woke up. They put a bandage on it. They gave me a suicide blanket and took everything from my cell. The thing I used to cut myself is gone, but I don't need it. I opened the skin and I can cut the artery with my fingernail. I can feel the pulse from it."

"Maybe we should have someone look at it," I said, because Jaber seemed to be in pain.

He nodded. I knocked on the nurses' station door and asked if we could get help. A young male nurse came out. He opened Jaber's bandage and I saw the wound—a gaping hole in the flesh. It ran about an inch across and went deep into Jaber's abdomen. The nurse began to pull something out of the hole, and for a second I thought it was Jaber's intestines. Realizing quickly that it was actually some kind of medical product, I told myself to relax. Jaber didn't need me to be hysterical.

"Yeah, we should get some new packing," the nurse said after he fished out about a foot of this strip. He filled the hole with new "packing" and put a bandage on it.

When the nurse left, Jaber said, "I wanted to do this before you came, but I needed to give you my will."

Still thinking about having seen the inside of Jaber's stomach, I thought some slightly tougher love might help.

"I'm not taking your goddam will," I told him. "You can give it to your family when you get home before Ramadan. Then they will know what to do when you die at ninety. Besides, I don't know anything about wills," I added with a little smile.

"I haven't done anything since March 11 last year. I kept thinking that I would go on the next flight, but it hasn't happened."

"It hasn't happened *yet*," I said. "That doesn't mean it won't happen. We're hearing better things than ever before. You have to wait! Just until Ramadan."

I didn't think I could get anything more out of him, but then he said, "Six days ago, I had a dream that I would go home in eighty days. That would be just before Ramadan."

"Why didn't you tell me about that? Wouldn't it be better to talk about that instead of about cutting arteries?" I asked with a smile.

"This morning I thought that maybe God doesn't want me to die."

"That seems like a safe bet," I said with a little laugh.

I talked more about the latest rumors from Bahrain and the things we had been doing to ratchet up the pressure. Jaber had heard all this a hundred times before, and he started talking again about how he had planned to sever his artery.

"They have watched me all the time for years, and I can still cut myself," he said.

We went back and forth like this for a couple of hours. I think that eventually I wore him out.

He said, "I will try to wait until Ramadan, inshallah. I don't think I will do anything until then. I'm sorry to my mom for doing this. She can't know."

"I understand. I won't say anything."

We had just a couple of minutes left. Jaber asked if I wanted to hear a joke. I had not seen that coming—a classic Jaber surprise.

"Yeah, I'd love to hear a joke."

"A man goes to a doctor for a blood test. They have trouble getting blood, so the nurse makes a little cut on his finger and sucks the blood out. The next day the man comes back to the doctor. They ask why, and he says he needs a urinalysis."

I laughed out loud, and so did Jaber. How did he come up with this stuff? And in this moment?

He turned serious again. "I will do my best. I will try to resist until Ramadan. If there is a ray of hope, we will hang on to it."

"That's all I can ask you to do. That's all your family can ask you to do."

Jaber looked at me. "I consider you a dear friend. Do your best."

Chapter 16

RAMADAN COMES EARLY

I flew back to New York on June 30, 2007, thinking maybe I had bought us a couple of months. But even if Jaber might hang on a bit more, I didn't want to think about what would come after that.

The following Monday, I went through my usual post-trip routine. I sent some information to Bahrain for the media. I called Jaber's and Isa's families with updates. I checked how far I'd gotten behind on billable cases and tried to find all my travel-related receipts for an expense report. It felt like a routine I'd been doing for years, likely because it was.

A few days later, Jaber's brother Amir called. He said someone from the Bahraini Ministry of Foreign Affairs had just contacted his uncle, unsolicited, to say Jaber would be home by Ramadan. The family was pressing for details, but that was an unprecedented call for us in and of itself. Immediately I wrote to Jaber, telling him about this outreach. I also mentioned that a *Washington Post* article based on his April 18 letter was set to run, and how much I had enjoyed sharing cheesecake. I hoped my correspondence might buoy his spirits for a day or two. And, really, the call was extraordinary.

But I reminded myself that getting our hopes up in connection with Guantanamo was no kind of formula for happiness.

On Monday, July 16, 2007, I woke up groggy after staying awake too late reading a Joe Strummer biography. I turned on my phone and saw far more emails than normal for an early Monday. One, from another Guantanamo lawyer, had a list of sixteen detainees who had just arrived in Saudi Arabia after being released. I deleted the email without looking at the list, figuring I wouldn't know the detainees by name.

I flicked through other messages and opened a second one from the same lawyer.

"Lucky thirteen? Isn't Jaber one of yours?" he wrote.

I scrolled down. "Jaber Mohammed" was number thirteen on the list. The hair on the back of my neck stood up. I felt lightheaded. Jaber was home? Should I believe it? I sat there, suddenly having no idea what to do.

My phone buzzed—a message from Nabeel Rajab: "Congratulations, brother. Mohammed is home."

It was almost too much to comprehend. Not wanting to be out of cell range even for a minute, I skipped the subway and took a cab to the office, despite interminable traffic. I called Jaber's brother Amir.

"Oh, Josh," he yelled into the phone with high-pitched giddiness. "It's a dream. He's home!"

I had a hundred questions.

Amir said that in the middle of the night he had gotten a call from a private number. He decided to answer. It was a very senior Saudi Interior Ministry official. The official told Amir that Jaber had just arrived in Riyadh. He invited the family to come. Amir called everyone else, starting with his mother, waking them all up. Nobody could believe it.

The government flew Amir, his mother, Jaber's daughter, and various siblings from Dammam in eastern Saudi to Riyadh, where they arrived at 2:30 a.m. Amir described a raucous family reunion of hugs and sobs. Jaber kissed his mom's hands and feet. Amir said Jaber looked very small. I knew exactly what he meant.

"Jaber called me a few hours after our visit," Amir told me. "He asked me to thank you for bringing cake . . . I can't remember the name of it."

"Cheesecake?"

"Yes, yes, that's it!"

We both laughed. It was just two weeks earlier that Jaber and I had devoured a Junior's cheesecake in Guantanamo.

"I really, really, really, from the bottom of my heart, want to thank you and Mark and everyone for everything you did for three years," Amir said. "I was really terrified when you told me about his last attempt, but now he is home. We need to stay in touch so we can see each other again. We don't want this to be it. You were Jaber's lawyer but my friend."

His voice was bubbling with feeling. I was choking up, listening to this kind, muscle-bound man whose family was intact again, albeit without his father.

At 11:12 a.m., I saw an email from our usual contact at the Department of Justice:

> I am writing to inform you that the United States has relinquished custody of petitioner Jaber Mohammed (ISN 361) and transferred him to the control of the Government of the Kingdom of Saudi Arabia.

A larger part of me than I should admit wanted to write back, "That's right, motherfucker! 361's home! We win, asshole!" But, likely, that's not the best aspect of my character, particularly for work purposes. More important, we still had a client at Guantanamo and would have to keep working with DOJ.

So, I said nothing to the government. Instead, I ran around the office, making sure everyone on the team had heard the news. I also wrote to firm management, telling them that Jaber was home.

"Great work—terrific news. Thank you," the firm's managing partner responded. Another wrote, "Thanks for the terrific work for Jaber!!"

A few minutes later, I saw an email from Walter Mondale in my inbox. That hardly happened every day. We had spoken a few times about the case, and he was someone who seemed to have no pretense, but I still wasn't nearly bold enough to have included him on my email to management. Instead, the firm's pro bono partner had forwarded my message to him.

"Dear Josh," he wrote. "This is a magnificent result. We are proud of what you have done and are doing. fritz mondale." This from the vice president of the first presidential administration to promote human rights explicitly. It was beyond cool.

There also were messages coming in from other habeas lawyers, all of whom were familiar with Jaber's story and had seen the news of his release. It was great to read them. One lawyer said, "This is wonderful, Josh, I am sure you are actually responsible for this, you were a one-man PR machine on his behalf." Another said, "That's great. You helped save this guy's life. I hope he is recovering."

The one that probably resonated the most actually came a few months later from an accomplished older lawyer whose seemingly effortless advocacy skills had been a marvel to watch:

> With all that's been going on I missed that Mohammed got out. You have my congratulations and deep admiration for that. The guy wanted to die, insisted on it, tried to kill himself before your eyes. Your tenacity, cussedness, and competitive heart simply would not let him. As I recall, the rhetoric about him was at the shrill end, with dark mutterings of war crimes. Now our government has shriveled up and slunk away without so much as a charge. It is down to you that he was alive to see it happen. It was lawyering of the first stripe—the achievement of a career.

On July 29, Amir called again. He said Jaber, who was in the Saudi rehabilitation program, would be able to take a call from me early the next morning Saudi time, which meant late that night my time. The idea of just picking up the phone and calling Jaber seemed crazy. But at 11:00 p.m., there he was at the other end of the line.

"Jaber, is that you?"

"Hey, Josh! It's good to hear you."

"I can't believe it."

"I can't believe it either."

"How are you?"

Jaber told me about the end of his time at Guantanamo. A few days before he left, he had asked to go to rec. A guard told him to wait because "Doc has something to tell you." They then took him to the detainee hospital. There, a colonel said, "Congratulations, you're going home. Saudi accepted you. It would take a little longer for Bahrain. I didn't think you'd want to wait."

Jaber's response was, "Saudi, Bahrain, India, it doesn't matter. I will go."

The colonel said Jaber had to sign a document, promising not to fight again for Al Qaeda. When Jaber said he hadn't fought to begin with, the colonel said Jaber didn't really have to sign, but it would be a gesture of goodwill if he did. Jaber figured he wasn't going to be fighting for anyone anyway, so he signed.

For the next four days in the Mental Health Unit, Jaber couldn't sleep. He thought he probably was going home but couldn't be positive.

He told me about the trip home, which by now I knew had been on a big Saudi government jet.

"361 was first on the plane. When I got on, it was like going from a cemetery to paradise. There were soldiers and Interior Ministry people, but they were so gentle. They smiled. They asked if I was okay. They asked if I wanted anything. They asked *me* if I wanted anything. They told me that everyone knew about me."

Based on bits and pieces he had learned, Jaber believed a Bahrain transfer had been in the works, but that the Saudi flight he took was leaving first, after having been delayed for a few months (he didn't know the cause of the delay). People wanted to get him out of Guantanamo as soon as possible, so he was added to that flight.

Jaber said that when he saw his family, everyone was crying. Amal said, "Daddy," which confused him because for a minute he thought she was his sister.

"I couldn't believe it. She's so much bigger. I just put my head on my mom's shoulder. She was holding me and touching my face and chest to make sure I was there. I told her, 'Mom, calm down. It's okay.'"

He continued, "From the deepest part of my heart, thank everyone who was worried. I will never forget any of them. When I heard people were concerned, especially in the US, it really made me feel better. Especially the nun who did the fasting."

"I know! We'll never forget the nun!" I said.

Jaber was talking about the plane ride again. "A new Jaber started on the airplane. A new everything. I forget everything. I forgave everybody—Muslim, Christian, anyone who was bad. Anyone who helped me, even guards, I won't forget forever."

For a minute I thought about PTSD and wondered how long Jaber's euphoria would last.

When our conversation paused for a minute, Jaber mentioned Isa. Left unsaid so far was the blunt reality that Isa was still at the base—our last client there. Jaber said he had come back to Saudi with people who had been in Camp 6, where Isa was held. They told him Isa was having a rough time, which I understood was a significant understatement. I told Jaber I would be writing to Isa right away and was sketching out dates for a trip. Obviously I didn't want to jinx anything, but I couldn't help hoping that trip would get mooted by a pre-Ramadan release.

I didn't say anything to Jaber about it, but I had wondered how his feelings toward me might change with his release. Unsolicited, Jaber let me know where he stood.

"Please thank the law firm for the help. They helped me a lot and the Bahrainis, especially when they put Joshua Colangelo-Bryan to follow my case. You have done very well for me. You were gentle and nice. You dealt with me brother-to-brother, not like an attorney. I remember each time you said, 'Just wait, be patient.' I thought 'I heard that before,' but now it's true. I miss sitting and talking with you. I will be your friend always."

Eventually Jaber said my phone bill was going to be huge, and he wanted me to save some money for another call. I looked at the clock. We had been on the phone for an hour and a half. We said our goodbyes, and I was about to hang up when I heard Jaber's voice.

"See you later, alligator," he said.

This time I nailed the response: "In a while, crocodile."

Chapter 17

LIFE AFTER (NEAR) DEATH

A few days after that phone call with Jaber, I heard from someone I trusted in Bahrain who reported that a source within the Bahraini government was saying Isa would go home soon. I wrote to tell Isa what I had heard, but I assured him we would keep pressing until he actually touched down in Manama.

As a person who never counts chickens before they've hatched—and grown up—it's not comfortable to think good things will happen. Still, it was hard not to feel that we were on a roll. Given the five releases we'd seen and the reports about a full Bahrain sweep by Ramadan, it felt almost like a foregone conclusion that Isa would be out quickly. Still, not wanting to jinx anything or be so optimistic that it would invite the universe to smite us, I tried to repress the hopeful feeling.

I didn't have to engage in those mental gymnastics for long. On August 9, 2007, I received an email from the government. Perhaps for the first time when seeing the "usdoj.gov" address in my inbox, I felt no anxiety. The email read, "I am writing to inform you that the United States has relinquished custody of petitioner Isa Ali Abdulla Almurbati (ISN 052) and transferred him to the control of the Government of Bahrain."

I felt disoriented, the way you do in a dream. For three years, Guantanamo had been the first thing I thought about in the morning and the last thing I thought about at night. It had been front of mind throughout the day. Trying to figure out what to do next had been my main preoccupation.

Now, unless I was missing something, that was it. There was nothing else to do. We were finished. Everyone was home. Sitting at my desk with the email still open, I was uncertain what to do or even quite how I felt, almost as if I was in a state of shock. I waited to feel joy, but it felt more surreal than joyous.

You have to appreciate this. You'll never get another moment like this if you work forty more years, I told myself. But while my mind understood the enormity of the moment, I didn't *feel* the enormity. Maybe it was too much to take in.

It was the same when I told Mark, Lauren, and Chris about the DOJ email. There were smiles, but it seemed as if we were trying to absorb the news rather than celebrating it. Also, it was impossible not to think about the hundreds of people still locked up at the base, which must have tempered our feelings.

Wanting to make it all feel more tangible, I sent an email to the habeas lawyer listserv, saying, "Isa Al Murbati, the last of our six clients to be at GTMO, made it home last night and was reunited with his family. There are no Bahrainis left at the base." It felt very satisfying to share that with the people who had been battling along with us and truly understood the significance of the news.

Late in the day, I saw a statement from Sheikh Amir Al Khalifa, the Bahraini minister of foreign affairs. He said Isa's release was the result of "efforts and directives" of King Hamad with the help of the prime minister and the crown prince—the three most powerful figures in Bahrain. The statement continued, "The issue of Bahraini detainees was always raised by Bahrain during visits to the United States, and it was at the forefront of discussions with the American administration." The statement also offered "thanks to the lawyers and civil society organizations which followed the plight of the

Bahraini Guantanamo detainees." I decided to interpret that as a thank you to us, at least in part.

In the days after Isa's release, a sense of joy continued to be elusive. When I thought about the prior three years, the positive feeling I mustered most often was satisfaction.

We had fought against a hugely powerful array of forces. There was the Bush administration, which created and defended the Guantanamo operation. There was Congress, which passed the Detainee Treatment Act and Military Commissions Act to kill our habeas cases. There were the courts, which weren't inclined to order meaningful relief for anyone at Guantanamo, given that the specter of 9/11 hovered over the cases. And there was a majority of the American public, which, perhaps still scarred by 9/11, saw nothing wrong with indefinite detention in Cuba even if it meant some innocent people were locked up. And abused.

On our side, we had a group of serious law firms along with some members of Congress and a bit of popular support. That hardly was a fair fight. Despite that, in our little case, we had gotten everyone home. When I framed it that way in my mind, it felt like a real accomplishment.

Of course, I had written to friends and family to tell them that Isa was home with the rest of our clients. In response, I heard from my high school girlfriend's mother, whom I had stayed in touch with over the years even after she moved to New Mexico.

"I'm at the Espanola library with tears in my eyes, feeling a bit foolish but what the hell," she wrote. "It's the last thing I expected to pull up today and I'm so happy for you. What a tremendous job you've done. Thanks that you never gave up on him."

In a way, that's what felt best. Despite odds that were long or felt impossible at times, we never stopped. We never quit just because we were outgunned by the government or because of Jaber's despair or because people wrote threats on message boards. I never even had thought of doing anything other than pushing forward. Not to say that I was unique among the habeas lawyers, but it still felt good to think I had always attacked every aspect of the case with everything I had.

That might have been part of the emotional ambivalence I was feeling. While I was trying not to focus on it, the moment I heard Isa was out, part of me had started wondering what I was going to do next. How was I going to find some other piece of work to replace Guantanamo, a case that combined deep personal relationships, helping people in the direst of straits, international diplomacy, media and public attention, and cutting-edge legal issues? How was I going to find something else that felt so important?

Because Guantanamo, like Kosovo before it, was not just a professional endeavor. It was something that worked its way into all parts of my life. It had provided clear purpose. It resolved any questions about what I was doing with my life. It gave me a hugely compelling external focus for just about all my energies and anxieties. I mean, it wasn't selfish to do the work, but it definitely wasn't selfless. No, it made *my* life better.

One answer to my questions about what to do next could have been to take on more Guantanamo clients. While most detainees had lawyers, there were plenty of people who could have used greater individual attention. Evidently the firm anticipated I might be thinking about that. Within a couple days of Isa's release, a member of management told me the firm was proud of what we'd accomplished but that we had played our part and would be leaving the rest to others. End of discussion.

Truthfully I wasn't sure I wanted to take on more habeas cases. The idea of forming entirely new relationships with people at the base—and all that potentially entailed—and cranking up again to battle the forces we'd been fighting for years was daunting emotionally. And maybe something new would be good. So, when the no-Guantanamo dictate was pronounced, I didn't fight back.

But I was anxiously expecting another conversation with the firm. I had spent three years not getting anywhere near my billable hour goals without any express agreement allowing for that. Now, with Guantanamo over, surely somebody would come to tell me to knock off all the pro bono. Whatever ambivalence I had about doing more Guantanamo work, the idea of returning to a standard billable practice was terrible.

I was thinking about whether I should try to propose something affirmatively when David Singer came to see me. He was a partner in the New York office who oversaw associate development at the time. He was a big proponent of pro bono in general and a booster of the Guantanamo work in particular, but I knew he also had to play the role of firm messenger.

"Do you want to get back on the partner track or stay with this niche you've created?" he asked.

I felt huge relief just hearing the question. Immediately I took the second option. David wasn't surprised. With little effort we hammered out an arrangement by which I took a salary reduction in exchange for being able to continue spending hundreds of hours per year on pro bono. It was an absolute no-brainer.

Jaber and I managed to talk a couple of times over the next few months while he was in the Saudi rehabilitation program. He told me that he wanted to look forward rather than dwell on the past, a theme the rehabilitation people seemed to urge. As someone who lives in the epicenter of psychotherapy—New York City—I worried about his trying to suppress Guantanamo trauma rather than face it. But I kept that to myself since Jaber and I only had quick calls, and I didn't want to offer advice contrary to what he was getting at the program.

Also, what did I really know? In Kosovo, people had experienced crimes against humanity and virtually none of them had access to therapy. I wasn't sure they were worse off emotionally than the average New Yorker who spends years in analysis talking about a withholding mother. Plus, Jaber seemed genuinely happy, particularly when he told me he had just driven a car for the first time since returning.

At the end of 2007, Jaber left the rehabilitation center and moved back to Dammam, his childhood hometown, where most of his family still lived. Initially he stayed with his mother. Then, with her and his brother, he bought a multifamily house for all of them to live in. Jaber was spending lots of time with his daughter. He began taking computer classes and eventually found a job in human resources at a private business. One of the bigger changes in his post-Guantanamo life came when he met and, in fairly short order, married a woman.

I was thrilled to hear about each development. At the same time, I wondered (or worried) again about whether Jaber would need to move away from our relationship and focus on a new life that was increasingly full. It turned out that he wanted to stay in touch, just as I did.

Early in 2008, we were talking when he said he was having trouble sleeping now and then. A few nights earlier, he had been tossing and turning when he got up and found a DVD labeled *United 93* next to the family television set. He hadn't known what the movie was about but started watching anyway. Quickly he realized it was the story of the plane that crashed in Pennsylvania after being hijacked on 9/11. He said he started to cry thinking about the terrible things people do to each other.

"He wants to be Christian, he wants to be Muslim, leave them alone," he said. "If I hear of anyone threatening violence, I will call Interior. It's bullshit to watch kids and women die. Just live with respect. Religion and color, leave them alone. People have destroyed Islam's reputation. It is not supposed to be violent. The Prophet, peace be upon him, lived with Jews and Christians. I don't have a problem with anyone. Deal with me respectfully and that's how I deal with you."

It was hard to argue. Of course, this was a conversation with Jaber, so inevitably it reverted to our special brand of humor. As we were getting off the phone, he said, "Josh, remember, don't choke your chicken." I had forgotten that he was a walking glossary of American slang. I laughed out loud. "Yeah, but it might help you fall asleep," I said.

During another call, he mentioned that his mother had asked about me. I told him my mother was always inquiring about him.

He asked for her email address, and they began a correspondence that I was copied on sometimes. At one point, she asked how he was, and he responded:

> HI dear Juliette
> now I can go anywere I want . . .
> and I can do anything I want . . .
> hwo wonderful the freedom . . .
> Iam living now in my home with my family and my doughter and my new wife in new life . . .
> nothing better than freedom. . . .
> nothing compare with the freedom . . .
> the freedom is the real life . . .
> believe me when I saying that I feel so happy when I receive an E_mail from you . . .
> I like to be friend with evrybody regadless what happend to me and what they did to me . . .
> I forgave evrybody wronged me . . .
> and I will be friendly till the last day in my life . . .
> I will keep my heart clean forever . . . freedom . . . kindness . . . friendship: this is my life.

Guantanamo stayed in the news although with less frequency than before. At one point, I saw a piece written by a former Guantanamo guard named Brandon Neeley. He had been at the base when detainees first arrived and had come to feel terrible about some of the things he had done. He wrote about having seen Jaber's IRF beating.

I told Jaber about the article and said I had a feeling that he and Brandon might both benefit from talking. Jaber didn't know Brandon by name and asked to see a photograph of him, which I emailed.

"He gave us a hard time," Jaber said after looking at the photograph, "but it is a new time now."

A few days later, after I had made contact with Brandon, the three of us were on the phone together.

"I was so young then," Brandon said, seemingly trying to explain himself. "They told us that everyone would kill us in a heartbeat."

"It made me feel very good when I heard you wanted to talk," Jaber replied. "When a guard wanted to know who I really was, it made me feel very good. When we got bad treatment from a guard we thought was a good American, it hurt worse than torture."

"The guards who started to realize that not everyone was a terrorist had no say-so," Brandon said. "I wish I had spoken out sooner."

"You still have a good heart if you want to talk now," Jaber said. "Remember that we weren't allowed to look you in the eye? We had no chance to express ourselves then."

"I remember that we always told you 'Look down, look down,'" Brandon replied. "I hope something I could say would give people who were detainees some comfort. I'm really sorry for what you had to go through."

Jaber grew more animated. "You're noble. This is very good. We can't live in the past. If we only think about the past and revenge, it is torture. You are taking a great step to explain that what happened was wrong."

Jaber remembered a guard who had taken him to the shower without shackles once. "I wish I had his email to thank him."

Brandon said he came from a small town in Texas and was told he'd be guarding the world's most dangerous men.

"Then I saw guys weighing 120 pounds who looked so weak. Before I got there, I thought they were crawling out of caves, but some of them listened to Eminem."

Jaber laughed.

I thought of an email Jaber had sent me with a still shot from *8 Mile*, the Eminem movie. It showed Eminem and several others in a car, all looking like tough guys. But a picture of George W. Bush's face had been swapped in for Eminem's. The caption read, "Life After the White House." It was a funny image.

At the end of the call, Jaber said, "It's good to talk to a guard without shackles."

"Yeah, like normal people," Brandon replied.

"It's finished now for us," Jaber said. "We need to move on."

Speaking of moving on, in March 2009, just over a year after Jaber left the rehabilitation center, he emailed me: "Dear Friend. I have good news. Allah gave me a very beautiful girl."

When I talked to Jaber, I told him I was thrilled. I also said I had an idea of how I might be able to visit him, even if it was a long shot. That was kind of our specialty, after all.

I had kept tabs on Bahrain out of personal interest since the Guantanamo case ended. While the country's human rights record had been bad historically, particularly in connection with the detention of political prisoners, things had seemed to improve during the early and mid-2000s. Unfortunately there were more recent reports of a resurgence in abusive interrogation techniques.

Always looking for a good pro bono project, I had approached Joe Stork, the deputy director for the Middle East and North Africa Division at Human Rights Watch. Joe had been covering Bahrain and the rest of the Middle East for years. His knowledge of the region was encyclopedic. He also was a kind and gracious person.

I told Joe I would go to Bahrain to investigate these new reports of abuse and, if warranted, draft a report for Human Rights Watch to publish—pro bono of course. Joe liked the idea so much that he said he would join me in Bahrain for at least the latter part of the investigation. We scheduled the trip for June.

In those years, it was very difficult for Westerners to get visas to enter Saudi, particularly if they weren't in the oil business or maybe high finance. I didn't think the Saudis were particularly likely to loosen their normal practices to let a lawyer see a former Guantanamo detainee. Still, Saudi was right next to Bahrain—and Jaber had just had a kid—so I needed to try.

I went to the Saudi consulate near the United Nations. There was a decidedly New York–looking guy whom I took to be doing security. I struck up a conversation with him and learned he was a retired detective from the New York Police Department. We chatted about the weather and the Yankees before he asked what brought me to the consulate. I said I was a lawyer who wanted to visit a former client. He didn't press for details, instead motioning to someone else who worked for the consulate, saying, "Hey, Mohamed, can you take care of this guy?"

About thirty minutes later, I had a five-year visa. I was stunned. Maybe it was just meant to be. Jaber could barely believe it when I told him.

The investigative trip to Bahrain was as intense as I had expected. I spent a week (the second half with Joe) interviewing people who reported that they had been tortured in detention centers and prisons. These reports were corroborated in many instances by visible injuries and in some instances by medical reports written by government doctors. Joe and I also met with government officials to get their side of the story (pure denials) as well as political opposition figures and human rights advocates.

Toward the end of the week, I started asking around for someone who could drive me to the Bahrain-Saudi border, which was at the end of a causeway linking the countries. Jaber would pick me up on the other side. But a local, surprised to hear I had a Saudi visa at all, asked to see my passport. He told me that the visa, written mostly in Arabic, specified that arrival was permitted only by air, not at a border crossing. This was news to me. I wondered if there even were flights between Bahrain and Dammam, where Jaber lived, since it was only about a forty-five-mile drive.

It turned out there were, and I quickly booked a ticket. When I got to the flight early the next morning, the waiting area was so packed I thought I must have gotten one of the last seats. I also thought I might have mistakenly gone to a gate for some kind of specialized tour that I wasn't on. Literally everyone else in the area was a young woman who, if I had to guess, was Filipina. I double-checked the flight number on the board behind the desk, confirming it was the right gate. As I thought about it, I figured this was a group of people going to be domestic workers in Saudi. Those positions are notoriously rife with abuse. Uselessly, I wished them well in my mind.

When we got off the plane in Saudi, there were separate lines toward immigration for men and women, which made my exit very quick, given the gender of all my travel companions.

The temperature was nearly 110 degrees outside the terminal where Jaber had said he would meet me. After a minute or two, a black Toyota pulled up. The driver got out. He had a beard and wore sunglasses. He also had a somewhat crazed-looking grin on his face.

I shifted my gaze, looking around for Jaber. But the man with the sunglasses growled, "Hey, get in," seemingly in my direction.

I came all the way from New York to Saudi and I have to deal with some weirdo here? I thought to myself.

Trying not to be too obvious, I took another quick look at the guy. It hit me. This was Jaber. Not only had I never seen him wearing anything other than a prison jumpsuit and shackles but he must have put on twenty-five pounds, making him a normal weight. And his highway-patrol shades hid part of his face.

"No way, not with you," I said, now playing along with his mock threat of "Get in."

"What, you think I'm crazy?" he asked, smiling even more crazily.

"I know you're crazy."

Jaber walked up to me and gave me a bear hug. For the first time, he felt solid.

"Welcome to Dammam. Now get in the car."

On the drive to Jaber's house, we kept looking at each other and saying things like, "This is crazy" and "I can't fucking believe it!" I also said, "How about slowing down, Sheikh?" as he zoomed through traffic. Somehow I had taken to calling Jaber "Sheikh" over the prior year or two, a bit of ironic humor he appreciated.

We got to Jaber's house. It was a modest and well-kept building of several stories. Jaber said Amir, his brother, was at work but would be home later. Jaber wasn't sure if his mom was ready for visitors yet as it was still early.

We walked up a couple of flights to Jaber's apartment. To a New Yorker, it was an enviable size and quite comfortable with a sitting room full of plush couches. I plopped down on one. But not for long.

Jaber had disappeared behind a door but now came back holding his baby daughter. He looked like an old hand with an infant. He held her out to me. I jumped up and took her, trying to make sure I supported her head. But she seemed to be doing just fine with that by herself. She was entirely calm as I held her, making an expression I took to be a smile.

As I swayed gently with his daughter in my arms, Jaber and I talked about what it was like for him to have another baby, some twelve years after his first. He said sleep had been in short supply. But he had a look of quiet contentment that spoke volumes.

There was a knock on the other side of the door that Jaber had come out from moments before. It was his wife. Jaber said she didn't feel comfortable meeting me face to face, given that I wasn't a relative. I had anticipated that might be the case, given traditional Saudi customs. But she and I spoke briefly from one side of the slightly opened door to the other with Jaber as interpreter. I told her that she had a beautiful baby and that I was sorry she didn't have a beautiful husband. She laughed, showing her sense of humor was a match for Jaber's. She thanked me for everything I had done for him.

As Jaber and I sat back down, a thought popped into my mind. "Where's Half Moon Beach?" I asked.

"Half Moon Beach?" he responded. "You know about that?"

"Don't you remember?" I asked. "Amir told me you went there as kids. It was one of the things he told me to say so you would trust me the first time I came to Guantanamo."

"I remember! Do you want to go?"

"Let's go," I said.

On the way down to the car, Jaber knocked on his mom's door. She came out wearing a hijab but nothing covering her face. She gave me a big smile and hug. Jaber, translating, said she considered me "a son," so it was not a problem for us to talk even without her being fully covered. I thanked her for the honor and said my mom felt the same about Jaber. She thanked me for getting him home and added that a big dinner would be served that evening.

Making clear that his driving style from the airport to his house hadn't been a fluke, Jaber tore toward Half Moon Beach in nearby Dhahran.

"It would be pretty silly if we die driving to a beach after all this," I yelled above the roar of the engine.

"You always worry too much!" Jaber responded.

"Yeah, but now I'm worried about *me*," I said only half joking.

We made it in one piece. The beach wasn't far from the road and had a little park next to it. The area had a seaside feel that was more Jersey shore than French Riviera.

As we walked, I tried to get a sense of how Jaber really was doing. I knew he always sounded pretty good on the phone, but I couldn't help worrying he had been burying all the Guantanamo crap and that it would come out in some terrible way at some point. He didn't resist the conversation and admitted that now and then he felt those Guantanamo experiences pulling him down. But he was determined to focus on the here and now or the future, and not the past.

"I wanted to forget all that when I got on the plane," he told me, echoing his intention since that very first time we talked after he got home.

A few minutes later, Jaber asked me to walk on ahead for a bit and then meet him back at the same place. I wasn't sure what was going on, but then I heard the call to a prayer that must have been emanating from several nearby mosques. I watched as Jaber joined a group of men for prayers out in the open near the beach. Clearly it was an established spot because everyone knew exactly where to go.

I watched for a moment or two before it felt like I was gawking. I started walking again. I thought about how it would have been impossible to predict when I was a kid that one day I would be near a beach in Saudi Arabia, strolling with a friend I had met at an American prison in Cuba. *It's a crazy story*, I thought. I felt grateful to be in it.

When we got back to the house, I ended up falling asleep on those plush couches. I'm not sure how long it was until I heard Amir and Jaber's uncle, whom I also knew, come in. I felt liberated to see them without having to provide an update from Guantanamo. Instead, we could talk just about the weather and work and sports like normal people. A few relatives I hadn't met soon arrived, as did another man who had survived Guantanamo. I knew his lawyer, and he asked me to send his greetings. Turned out, it was dinnertime.

We sat on the floor in a circle just in time for the food, which started coming in waves. I could barely keep track of the courses and dishes, all of which were fantastic.

I paused eating at one point just long enough to ask Jaber over the din of conversation, "Where's the McDonald's Filet-O-Fish with extra mayonnaise? Where are the M&Ms?"

Jaber laughed. Amir did too. Over the years I had told Amir how Jaber refused anything but junk food during our visits.

"No McDonald's in my mother's kitchen," Jaber said. "But you remember what we said we would eat together?"

"Cheesecake?" I asked, not sure what he was getting at.

"No cheesecake. You'll see."

A few minutes later, the next set of plates arrived. I saw what Jaber was talking about. It was molokhia, the Egyptian dish with broth, rice, and chicken that we had discussed during our first meeting. Steam from the dish carried its aroma to us. Jaber's eyes lit up as he looked first at the stew and then me.

"You remember all the times you told me to hold on?" Jaber asked quietly. "Remember you told me Guantanamo wasn't forever and if I didn't hurt myself, we would eat molokhia together here?"

I nodded. I will always remember feeling like I was out on the highest and weakest limb when offering those promises. Looking at Jaber and eating his mother's molokhia, it felt great to know I had made good on them.

EPILOGUE

Jaber continues to live happily with his wife and kids, having added to the brood several times since I held his baby in Saudi. He works in human resources for a private company. Although I suspect he's gotten a speeding ticket or two, he hasn't had any other trouble since arriving home. And despite my worrying about Jaber's repressing trauma, he truly seems to have put his years in Guantanamo behind him in a way that's nothing short of remarkable.

I have two stepkids and a teenage daughter who keep me on my toes and a spouse who keeps me grounded. After over twenty years of my hybrid pro-bono-billable arrangement, the firm decided that "profits per attorney" was really the only metric that matters. Obviously that didn't reflect well on me, so I moved on to Human Rights First, where I do impact litigation as well as human rights investigations and advocacy. Not thinking about billable work and doing cases only because they're worth it is a blessing.

Jaber and I are still in touch. We don't spend much time talking about isolation or abusive interrogation techniques anymore, which is terrific, except it leaves more space for Jaber to give me a hard time—something he has never tired of. Recently he was reminding me that I'm too serious and a "tightwad" to boot.

Someday I'll have to track down the guard who taught him that expression . . .

The detention operation remains open at Guantanamo. As of this writing, there are fifteen people locked up as "enemy combatants" at an estimated cost of over $13 million per person annually. The government has charged the most well-known individuals in this group with crimes; however, those trials haven't even started because the Bush administration created an inadequate ad hoc court system at Guantanamo that has seen repeated missteps and legal challenges. And, as if Guantanamo's existence hasn't been a moral, strategic, and legal disaster for over two decades, in 2025, the Trump administration began using the prisons at the base to house migrants being deported from the US. Those stays were so short that, effectively, they have been the most expensive stopovers in history. Undoubtedly the administration thinks the cruel theater of it is worth every penny.

ACKNOWLEDGMENTS

I have to express my deep gratitude to Tracy Aanenson and Humanitas Media. Without Tracy's vision and commitment, this book would never have come to be.

A special thanks to Allen Peacock for his expertise in shaping and tightening the book.

I am grateful to Rick Moody, Barbara Jones of the Stuart Krichevsky Literary Agency, Eden Wurmfeld, Rob Boynton, Ashima Aggarwal, Jeremy Townsend, Emily Wichland, David Wilk, Megan Posco, Jacqui Daniels, and Lauren Rasmus for their help and encouragement along the way.

To my parents and step-parents who may not have always agreed on much, but all of whom believe deeply in trying to help others.

To Sarah—when she said, in her understated way, that a draft of the book was "good," I knew I could show it to other people. To Naya, Rhea, and Will for keeping me even more humble than I would feel otherwise.

And to Jaber, for hanging in there when it was the hardest, and for really living life now that he can.

INDEX

N

O

P

R

ABOUT HUMANITAS MEDIA

Where Human Rights Meet Human Stories

Humanitas Media was born from a belief in storytelling as a force for human rights. We amplify personal narratives that expose injustice, affirm dignity, and empower survivors to reclaim their voices. By confronting systems of oppression and lifting marginalized perspectives, our mission is to connect powerful human stories with a global audience. We are committed to making these narratives accessible and emotionally resonant—building empathy and deepening awareness. Through these deeply human stories, Humanitas Media will inspire a global community, embracing understanding and solidarity. Find out more at humanitasmedia.org, and follow us on Instagram (@humanitas_media) and Facebook (Humanitas Media).